Norman Williams Bingham

**The Book of Athletics and Out-Of-Door Sports**

Containing Practical Advice and Suggestions from College Team Captains and Other

Amateurs

Norman Williams Bingham

**The Book of Athletics and Out-Of-Door Sports**
*Containing Practical Advice and Suggestions from College Team Captains and Other Amateurs*

ISBN/EAN: 9783337076153

Printed in Europe, USA, Canada, Australia, Japan

Cover: Foto ©Andreas Hilbeck / pixelio.de

More available books at **www.hansebooks.com**

# THE BOOK OF ATHLETICS

AND

## OUT-OF-DOOR SPORTS

CONTAINING PRACTICAL ADVICE AND SUGGESTIONS FROM COLLEGE
TEAM-CAPTAINS AND OTHER AMATEURS, ON FOOT-BALL,
BASE-BALL, TENNIS, ROWING, GOLF, SPRINT-
ING, BICYCLING, SWIMMING, SKAT-
ING, YACHTING, ETC.

EDITED BY
NORMAN W. BINGHAM, Jr.

*ILLUSTRATED BY G. W. PICKNELL AND OTHERS*

BOSTON
LOTHROP PUBLISHING COMPANY
1895

## PREFACE.

In compiling this "Book of Athletics," no attempt has been made to produce an exhaustive treatise on every branch of sport now popular with the boys and girls of America. The design has been, rather, to give to those who are interested in, and have some knowledge of, the principal out-of-door sports the benefit of the experience and observation of those who have spent considerable time in their pursuit. Discussions which would be intelligible and of interest only to experts, as well as definitions and descriptions for the benefit of the wholly uninitiated, have been generally avoided.

In the list of games, no pretence has been made of including all that are practised at the present time: the intention has been to include those which have a strong hold on popularity, such as foot-ball, base-ball, rowing, tennis, cricket, swimming, skating, and the like.

Several forms of sport not properly included under the term "athletics," but which are eminently desirable for the recreative exercise they furnish, have been thought worthy of a place in a book which aims quite as much to awaken and increase a healthy interest in out-of-door life as to point the way to absolute excellence in competition. At the same time, it is felt that the advice offered by such authorities as Messrs. Bancroft, Dwight, Cumnock, Bliss, Mapes, and others, cannot but be of interest to all lovers of sport.

The descriptive article on "Knots, Hitches, and Splices" has been included as a valuable adjunct to the paper on "Yachting."

# TABLE OF CONTENTS.

| Chapter. | | Page. |
|---|---|---|
| I. | The Use and Abuse of Athletics | 9 |
| | By the Editor. | |
| II. | Advice to School Foot-Ball Captains | 21 |
| | By Arthur J. Cumnock. | |
| III. | Handling a College Nine | 33 |
| | By Lawrence T. Bliss. | |
| IV. | Seven Good Rules for Base-Ball Players to bear in Mind | 40 |
| | By W. S. Martin, Jr. | |
| V. | A Sermon on Lawn Tennis | 42 |
| | By James Dwight. | |
| VI. | How to train a Crew | 56 |
| | By William A. Bancroft. | |
| VII. | Cricket as played in America | 75 |
| | By Ralph Cracknell. | |
| VIII. | Golf: the Coming Game | 88 |
| | By Hugh S. Hart. | |
| IX. | About Bicycles | 96 |
| | By Kirk Munroe. | |
| X. | Running and Hurdling | 107 |
| | By Norman W. Bingham, Jr. | |

## TABLE OF CONTENTS.

| Chapter. | | Page. |
|---|---|---|
| XI. | Hare and Hounds Runs. | 121 |
| | By David W. Fenton, 2d. | |
| XII. | Hints for Young Pedestrians | 128 |
| | By Charles M. Skinner. | |
| XIII. | Out-of-Door Gymnastics | 146 |
| | By John Graham. | |
| XIV. | How to make an Out-Door Gymnasium | 156 |
| | By William F. Garcelon. | |
| XV. | Hints for Yachtsmen | 164 |
| | By Julius A. Palmer, Jr. | |
| XVI. | The Art of Swimming | 190 |
| | By Harry E. Rose. | |
| XVII. | Sport in the Water | 203 |
| | By Alexander Black. | |
| XVIII. | A Cane Rush | 225 |
| | By Malcolm Townsend. | |
| XIX. | Hurdling | 238 |
| | By Herbert Mapes. | |
| XX. | The Running Broad Jump | 252 |
| | By E. B. Bloss. | |
| XXI. | Skating | 259 |
| | By Charles R. Talbot. | |
| XXII. | Hand-in-Hand Skating | 267 |
| | By W. G. Van T. Sutphen. | |
| XXIII. | Knots, Hitches, and Splices | 280 |
| | By Charles R. Talbot. | |
| XXIV. | Summer Sports | 295 |
| | By the Editor. | |
| Index | | 315 |

# THE USE AND ABUSE OF ATHLETICS.

### BY THE EDITOR.

EVERY healthy boy likes to be out of doors; and almost every boy is, at some period in his life, an enthusiast on the subject of athletics. Every sane man is ready to allow that a certain amount of out-door life and exercise is desirable, — a tonic to both mind and body, and, on the whole, quite essential to a well-ordered existence. But on the value of competition, the grown men are hardly as ready to agree as are the boys.

There are some, to be sure, who, bidding for popularity with youth, are ever willing to overlook excesses. With "Boys will be boys," or "Wellington's armies were trained on foot-ball fields," they meet all objections raised against athletics, and end by saying impressively, "*Mens sana in corpore sano,*" quite taking it for granted that the *mens sana* will be there any way. They talk as they do because it is easier and pleasanter to let evils exist than to attempt to reform them. They should not, and I believe do not, enlist any great measure of respect from sensible boys.

Then, there are the chronic grumblers, though luckily their number is small. These men, having forgotten that they were ever boys, or perhaps never having been real boys, fume and rant, and give you to understand that all time spent in the field or on the water is worse than wasted. Feeling themselves that, sooner or later, the world must look dark to every one, they would hurry the natural course of things by forcing boys and girls to wear smoked glasses. Their opposition to athletics is prejudiced, abusive, and often absurd. They are more deserving of pity than of anything else.

But there is still another class of the older men who have the real welfare of the boys close at heart; by them the athletic craze which has possessed the country during the past few years has been observed with no little apprehension. They shake their heads, and rightly, at the all-too-marked difference between the zeal with which the boy of to-day enters into his games, and the listlessness with which he performs the more serious tasks which his school duties bring him. They are not, like the grumblers, hostile to all that is bright and pleasure-producing; but they do realize that, when what should be a means becomes an end, something is going wrong. They find a boy in the class-room working out foot-ball problems on the fly-leaf of his algebra, looking at no part of the daily papers except the sporting-pages, sometimes almost deifying a favorite pitcher or half-back, and they wonder what the end of all this is going to be. They ask themselves if, on the whole, the good that comes from athletics is not more than outweighed by the evil; and they do not always find at once an easy answer to the question.

Now, between those who enter into competition solely for the sake of winning a prize or a victory, and those who love the sport for its own sake, there has always been a distinction. The word "athlete" found its derivation in a name which was applied to those old Greeks who strove for prizes in the games. It was never used to designate those who daily practised in the gymnasium from love of exercise pure and simple. The athlete of that time, however, did not think one quarter as much about the prize itself as about the glory that went with victory, which was very great. We have all read with some wonder of how a Greek town would make a breach in its walls at the home-coming of its victorious representative, and would erect a statue to his honor. But, after all, the esteem which is paid to some young athletes to-day is scarcely less extravagant, and, were we not used to hearing of it, might sound nearly as strange.

What, then, it may be asked, is the justification, if any, for the intense interest in these games, and the spending of so much time and money in their pursuit? Do not the "highly competitive" sports, as compared with the lighter games and those out-of-door pursuits which are purely recreative, receive proportionately too great an amount of attention? Probably they do, and yet some of the benefits they bring with them are so undoubted that they cannot be lightly disregarded.

The average American boy is of rather a high-strung and nervous temperament. He likes action; he wishes to be doing something, and, quite naturally, prefers that something to be anything rather than real work. Very fortunately the greater part of his superfluous energy finds its escape through his devotion to athletic sports. Fortunately, I say, for in thus harmlessly gratifying his appetite for excitement he involuntarily learns many a useful lesson.

First of all, he learns, when he trains for a team, what it is to be subject to discipline. He readily and willingly imposes on himself many hardships, because he sees that they are necessary if he would succeed. He is at an age when there is something which he can do as well as any one, even though that something is only athletics. For once he becomes interested, and works with enthusiasm, — an enthusiasm which, if it is mistaken, must nevertheless gain the respect even of those who see its folly. If this sometimes leads him into error, he should be set right, but not necessarily deprived of his sport.

Perseverance, otherwise known as "sand," is another thing of which a boy soons learns the value. He sees that he must fight hard to the very end, every time, if he is to accomplish anything. The "quitter" never amounts to much; and this fact the boy who undertakes the practice of any form of athletics must quickly recognize. It is hard to see how this steady pegging away in the face of all discouragements can fail to have its influence in making a more valuable lot of men.

Aside from the effect on the disposition, there is of course the physical good which comes from regular exercise. It will probably be argued that the exercise could as well, or better, be taken without the strain of severe competition. This is perfectly true; and the only question is, Would it? It is doubtful if, without the incentive of the competition, it would be possible to get anything like the number of young men to take regular exercise that now do so. Once one has formed the habit, however, it is noticeable that he will generally arrange to spend a certain amount of time in the open air long after he has given up regular games and training. To know the blessedness of being in perfect condition is enough to make any one feel that, in training or out, it is worth while to take care of himself.

And yet the evils which are charged to athletics are not all imaginary. Not even the warmest enthusiast can claim that. The point which perhaps is responsible for the greatest number of strictures is the question of interference with studies or work, concerning which one hears a great deal of worth-

A Championship Game.
(By permission of Pach Bros., New York, Cambridge, and New Haven.)

less talk. It is easy, on one hand, to show that the hours occupied in getting to the grounds and back, and going through the daily training, are no more than every boy ought to spend in such a way; and it is equally easy to turn around and point to numerous cases where boys do neglect their studies for athletics. Considering the question calmly, it seems perfectly evident that, as a rule, the boys who take active part in any of the games do devote too much time to them. But this is because a great amount of time is wasted. Boys will linger about, long after they are through practising. They let their attention wander off to the field when other subjects have claims upon it. This is a bad habit, not alone from the standpoint of the instructor, but also from that of the athlete. "Over-training" is well known to result from mental as well as physical causes; and he who lets himself brood constantly over the games he is to play, or the races he is to run, will more than likely soon find himself growing "stale." It is perfectly possible to take part in athletics, and to do the rest of one's school work properly; and when every boy who is a lover of out-of-door sports makes up his mind to demonstrate this statement, the objections will cease.

The trickery and deceit which are countenanced in some games — which, indeed, are sometimes considered a part of them — are all wrong. The games should breed manliness and generosity, not treachery and cunning. Yet we find that, in baseball, boys who in most things are the soul of honesty will cut across from first to third base if the chance offers, will claim to have caught a ball " on the fly," which they know to have touched the ground, and will do many other things which are simply dishonest. There is certainly a danger that such loose standards may in time be applied to the rest of a boy's living. What is wanted is the nobler spirit of " fair play."

Athletics, as they are, doubtless tend in many cases to distort a young boy's estimate of the desirability of physical as compared with intellectual and moral force. This tendency can best be counteracted by a determined effort on the part of the boys who have grown up. They must try to keep in touch with the younger generation, set things right where they go wrong, and, above all, prevent boys who lack stability of character from becoming leaders.

Meanwhile, the tremendous and irrational excitement which has been customary at the time of our more prominent athletic contests seems to have reached its limit, and already there are signs of a healthy reaction. The result of this reaction will doubtless be to force athletics to the field they should occupy — a systematic means of physical development. Incidentally, an increasing interest in sport for sport's sake may be aroused. As the number of spectators at a big game diminishes, so may the number of people exercising increase. Competition is a good thing, but it may be carried too far. Moderation seems to be what is most needed at present.

What we have to look forward to, then, is not the arranging of more "championship" games, which draw from ten thousand to thirty thousand people to see them, but a more careful and more intelligent caring for the bodily welfare on the part of a larger number of people. Most men do not take as good care of themselves as they do of their dogs and horses. Athletics, rightly used, will tend to counteract this carelessness.

It would be well if every boy were to set up for himself a standard of manhood to which he would like to attain. Let him remember that strength and power are the results of generations of temperance and right living, and that in taking the best of care of himself a boy is, at least, doing his share toward the realization of a race of stronger men and more beautiful women.

# ADVICE TO SCHOOL FOOT-BALL CAPTAINS.

### BY ARTHUR J. CUMNOCK,
*Captain of the Harvard Foot-ball Teams of 1889 and 1890.*

*Running and Warding Off.*

THE average school, with small numbers and only a few large boys to pick from, is at a disadvantage when pitted against one of the great schools, such as Exeter, Andover, Groton, St. Marks, or Lawrenceville. But in foot-ball, skill and spirit will take the place of weight and brute force every time.

Every school captain is anxious to work, but perhaps does not know where to begin or how to develop his team. The game seems to be formidable and intricate at first, and one is apt to begin at the wrong end. Instead of planning "touchdowns" and big scores, you must begin at the foundation; you must creep before you can walk. On this foundation, so often neglected, everything depends; without it you cannot hope for team play or success.

In order to make clear what is meant by foundation, let us look at a few practical facts.

A team cannot make ground against an equally good team, unless it can "block;" and, *vice versâ*, an eleven cannot stop an opponent from advancing the ball, unless it can get through and tackle. A team's offensive play depends almost entirely upon the accuracy with which the centre rush passes the ball to the quarter-back; on the ability of the quarter to pick the ball up, however badly it may come back, and pass it accurately to the runner; on the ability of the halves to run strongly, dodge, use the arm, and catch the ball; on the blocking off of the team, and the runner's ability to take advantage of it. When a team is pressed to the last extremity, it depends upon a sure kick. A game has often been saved by a safe catch or a quick fall on the ball after a muff.

These few examples will serve to show you that every movement in foot-ball depends directly upon several details. Such details are what make up the foundation, and on their perfection depends good team play.

I can best illustrate what is meant by "team play," and its relation to these details, by asking

The Snap Back.

you to imagine a board in which eleven ink-wells have been imbedded. Pour ink into each of these wells. Then as you pour a little more into every one, they overflow their edges till the overflow of each meets the overflow of its neighbor, and the board is covered. If you should neglect to pour the "little more" into any well, the overflow of the others would have to cover its part, and the total covering would be just so much thinner.

So when each boy on a foot-ball eleven conquers

the duties of his own position, he can enlarge his sphere of action till he meets the rest of the team doing the same thing; then the relations between the different positions can be perfected, one boy helping another, till the whole team takes a part in every play. The mastery of these details is often neglected; and when the time comes for the eleven to exert itself as a unit, each player is so much occupied in "filling his own well," that he cannot give any strength or attention to the rest of the team, but leaves it to the other ten.

The aim of every captain is to have his team play as one man; and this is evidently dependent on the strength and resources his players are able to give to a concentrated effort. So he may well study into everything that will tend toward this end.

Every detail of foot-ball is a problem which may be solved by study. These details must be studied out of the field, however, and the solutions put to a test during practice games. To solve these difficulties on the field you will find is as perplexing as to learn an arithmetic or geometry lesson out there.

Take, for instance, blocking and getting through. There are a great many ways of doing these things, and you cannot find them all out in a minute or two; you must live with them. Think out ways, invent new methods, and then try them. Do not make them too complicated, and do not get discouraged because something you thought was good "doesn't work." No two boys are of the same size, strength, quickness, or mental capacity; and what one boy can do well, another would find himself unfitted for. Each boy's qualities must be studied into to get the best results. For instance, Newell, the old Harvard player, used to get through as well as, if not better than, any one in the country. Some one at Yale understood this, and invented a new way to stop him. Winter, who was his opponent, stood back a yard or two and let Newell start first. As he was going by, Winter and Bliss, a half-back who stood near, threw their weight on him from an angle, and either pushed him back or blocked him off.

Punting.

Tackling is only a knack, and can be studied as well as wrestling. For instance, S. V. R. Crosby, Harvard '91, an end-rush, could not tackle; and it was almost impossible to explain the way to do it. Finally a bag was hung up, on which was a projection representing an arm, so he could not tackle high. This bag was swung for Crosby to get the knack of ducking, taking hold, and throwing. He studied it all out, and in three or four days he tackled beautifully.

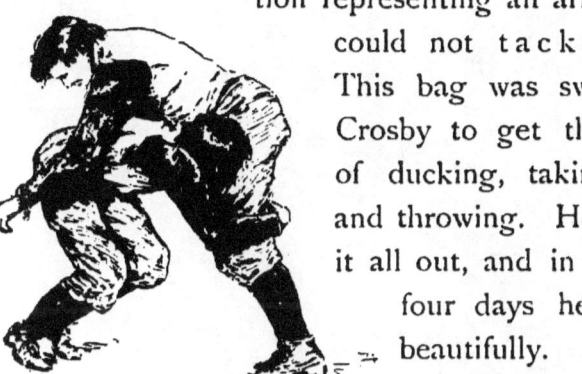

*Tackling.*

Practice off the field will enable the centre-rush to pass the ball correctly to the quarter every time. By passing for an hour a day during the summer, a quarter-back will find that he can handle a foot-ball as easily as he can a base-ball, and throw it as accurately. If he follows the ball, trying to get into imaginary plays when he is practising, in a regular game he will keep up with the ball, and be able to block off for the runner.

A back's duties require skill and accuracy for every movement, and there is no limit to the possibilities of his position. He can work up kicking, catching, running with a ball, using his arm, and,

Warding off Tackle.

among many other things, how to take advantage of blocking off.

During one whole summer, Everett Lake, the Harvard half-back, practised warding off tacklers with his arm. When autumn came he was one of the most difficult halves in the country to stop, because, in addition to his great weight and strength, the tackler was nearly always kept at arm's length.

The kicking of Captain Trafford of the Harvard '91 and '92 elevens illustrated what study and hard work can do for a full-back. In July, in the summer before he came to college, he could not drop-kick at all. Part of a week was spent in simply studying the way to make a drop-kick. He worked an hour or two every day during the summer; and when he came to college in the fall, he could drop the ball from the thirty-five yard line between the goal-posts nearly every time.

When a captain gets so that he is able to reason these details out, and when his team sees how easy it is for them to settle any difficulty by study, they are on the road to success. I know of a team that was said to have coached itself; this simply means they played foot-ball not like so many machines, but like thinking and reasoning beings.

During the practice game, when a misplay is discovered, do not blame the team without telling them how to overcome it. Put them back in the positions they were in when it happened, and the trouble will soon appear. Then show them the way to prevent it; and if you do not happen to know, do not be ashamed to study it out with them.

The spirit of a team is another important element. An eleven going into a match with great skill and a thorough knowledge of the game possesses a confidence that is half the battle. In selecting the boys for your team, give preference to those who are honest hard workers; avoid "stars," who save

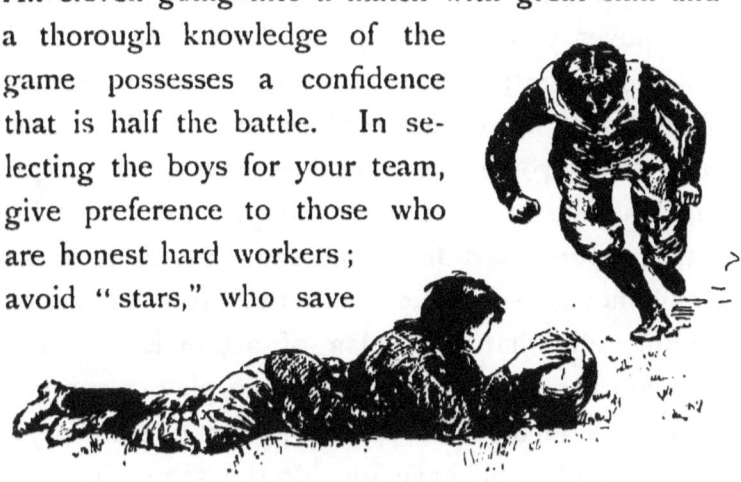

*A Try for Goal.*

themselves from the regular team work for startling individual plays. A Harvard captain was once giving his last instructions to the team before a Yale game. Turning to the end-rushers he said,

"I shall hold you alone responsible for being down on the ball every time after a kick;" when the centre-rush, whose duty it was to block, and who had little chance to do anything else, said, "I am going to be down there too." And he was. He did his own blocking, and was often down the field before the ends got there. That kind of spirit will win a victory every time.

You will find, in executing the different plays and moves you may plan, that the matter of detail still occupies a prominent position. You may tell a player to go to a certain place; but to obtain the best results you must show him how he is to go, and what he is to do when he gets there. Make your players start from the same positions in as many moves as you can, so that your opponent cannot tell what your plan of action is; in this way you can pass quickly from one play to another without a change of position. Make each boy's duties simple, and have him do the same thing in as many moves as possible. Do not waste your time on complicated tricks; team play is absolutely necessary for success. This comes from developing the players and their positions from the foundation up, and not from attempting intricate moves with boys who do not understand the rudiments of the game.

Make your signals simple, easy to be remembered, and at the same time effective. A complicated code of signals will puzzle your own side, when excited, quite as much as it does your opponents.

In conclusion, study the details of each position of your eleven, and develop your players so they may have resources at their command. Show them the relations between the

*Falling on a Muff.*

different positions, and teach them to play into each other's hands. Your reward will be that in every movement, from making a hole to stopping an end play, you will have eleven players concentrated, who know how to play together for the same end.

This is a hard kind of a team to beat, for they make few misplays themselves, and know how to take advantage of their opponents' errors.

# HANDLING A COLLEGE NINE.

### BY LAWRENCE T. BLISS,
#### Captain of the Yale Base-ball Team of 1893.

Hip Exercise.

FOR the last few years the game of base-ball, in colleges and universities, has lost much of its popularity, and has given way to foot-ball, which, as now played, is practically a new game.

The reason is that base-ball is more or less in the hands of professionals, while foot-ball is as yet entirely free from what one would call "professionalism."

This article is written from a college point of view, and is designed to tell the young base-ball enthusiasts something concerning the handling and training of a base-ball team in one of our American colleges.

As soon as the foot-ball season is over, the captain and manager of the base-ball team decide as to their plans for the coming season. These include

*Knee Exercise.*

the number of games that shall be scheduled away from home, and also the home games, planning for the Easter trip, obtaining a competent man to coach the candidates for pitcher, and many other minor details that scarcely need mention here.

No regular training is commenced until about the first of February, when all candidates are requested to present themselves at the gymnasium.

The first training is an average daily afternoon run of from a mile and a half to two miles; after this the candidates go to the "cage." In this building the candidates assemble, and go through a variety of movements designed to limber up the muscles; these exercises include moving the body up and down, keeping the back straight, and

*Back Exercise.*

bending the knees; then, bending the back from the hips, with arms straight out from the shoulders, and trying to touch the ground without bending the knees; raising one's self on tiptoes, revolving the arms in a circle in front of the chest, first in one direction, then the opposite; and finally, with hands on hips, moving the body from one side to the other.

*The Pitcher.*

On Wednesday and Saturday afternoons, these being half-holidays, the training work commences earlier. Before taking the accustomed run, a few grounders are knocked to each man, the benefit being very great, as it teaches a player to handle himself well, even though he is an outfielder. Outfielders have quite a number of grounders to stop during the season, and many games have been lost through the inability of some of the men to stop

*The Catcher in Armor.*

such balls. This practice also limbers the player's throwing arm, as he throws nearly the length of the cage. It is also a great help to a captain, as it is the only way in which he is able to test, weed out, and get rid of some of his superfluous material. For these reasons, too, it is well to practise picking up grounders even in a gymnasium with a wooden floor, if a school team is deprived of the advantages of a cage.

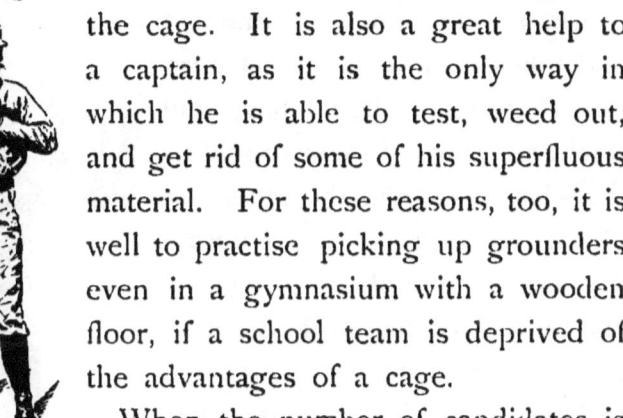
*Watching Bases.*

When the number of candidates is reduced a little, and the days grow longer, the Wednesday and Saturday afternoon practice is taken up daily, and base sliding is added.

Base sliding on the hard ground in the cage requires a good deal of nerve for a man who has never slid head first before. Even if he has the required nerve, he is often liable to injure himself. For this reason Mr. Stagg, a former captain of the Yale base-ball team, invented a sliding machine, which consists of a wooden frame with a heavy piece of carpet stretched tight across it. This is so placed that the carpet rests upon the ground. After a few lessons on this, the new men slide on the ground without fear of being hurt.

About the first of March the coach arrives, and takes charge of the pitchers. A college team should have four pitchers. Two of them should be first-class ones, and the other two above the average. It is always a good thing to have an eye on the future in selecting and coaching pitchers; for a college, sooner or later, has to lose its star players, as graduation day comes around and the senior is no longer an undergraduate.

*The First Baseman.*

There are many different opinions in regard to the advantages and disadvantages of using a cage to practise batting in. It has many disadvantages for this particular use. The light is apt to be very poor; the space too small. Because of these two drawbacks the eye is compelled to follow the ball in an enclosure with a background. When he is in the open field the player will find what a difference this makes. A good example of these disadvantages was seen in the Harvards' heavy batting team of

1891. They did not use the cage to practise batting in, although they have an excellent one.

But, on the other hand, this cage practice is excellent in giving a man batting form, and practice in swinging the bat. The cage is invaluable also for battery practice.

It is very seldom that a team can obtain more than a week's out-door practice before the Easter trip; so by the end of March, which is the time that the Easter trip commences, the team is very rusty. About fifteen or sixteen men are taken on the trip, and a game is arranged for every

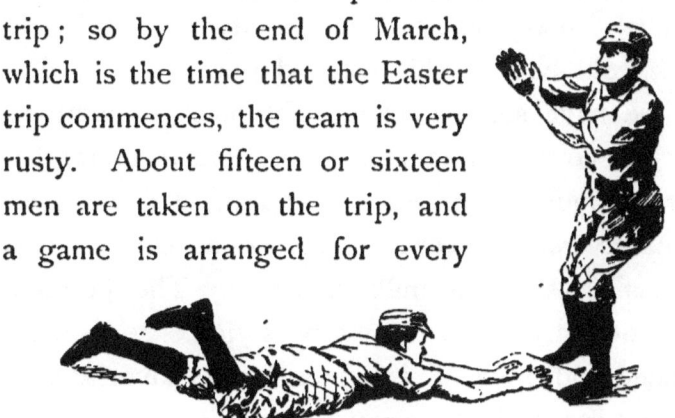

*Sliding for Base.*

day. These games, as a rule, are against professionals. After a week's play the team returns home, and plays two or three games a week during the remainder of the season. The work at the field every afternoon, except when a game is scheduled, consists of an hour's batting and a half-hour's fielding, a little base sliding, and fifteen or twenty minutes' team practice.

It might be well to say a few words here concerning table diet when training for base-ball. The old custom was to feed the different athletic teams on nothing but rare beef and potatoes. Now, however, the bill of fare consists of wholesome food with quite a variety. For breakfast we have fruit, oatmeal, steak, omelet, and potatoes; for lunch, steak, cold beef or chicken, and potatoes; for dinner we have soup, chicken, beef, mashed potatoes, pease or corn, and tomatoes, with bread, tapioca or custard pudding for dessert, and twice a week we have ice-cream. Toast is served at every meal; oatmeal water and milk to drink. The potatoes are cooked in nearly every style except fried. Hashed and browned is generally the favorite way. So, you see, training is not starving.

This brief statement of training, though referring to college base-ball work, may also be of suggestion and use to boys who are going in for a course in base-ball, and wish to make their home club strong and successful players.

# SEVEN GOOD RULES FOR BASE-BALL PLAYERS TO BEAR IN MIND.

### BY W. S. MARTIN, JR.

*Captain of the Tufts College Base-ball Team of 1893.*

ONE. — Base runners must always remember and turn to the right of the foul line in returning to first, when they have overrun that base.

Two. — Batters should run whenever they touch the ball, or whenever they have struck three times and missed it. No matter if two men are out, you may not be the third one if you run well.

THREE. — It would be well for young players to remember and keep a base runner on the third base, if the opposing catcher is weak up under the bat, or if the opponent's pitcher is wild.

FOUR. — To be a good batter you must stand up to the plate fearlessly, and the ball must be met by the weight of the body instead of the swing of the arms. This can be done by resting on one leg, so that you can easily step forward to meet the coming ball.

Five. — Infielders should always run out to help the outfielders, on the throw in of a hard-batted ball. This may save a run.

Six. — Always play for the advancing man. If there is a man on first, the ball when hit should be played to second and then to first base. If there is a man on first and second, the ball should go to the third base, and then to second.

Seven. — Captains should always strive to perfect their team play. It is what wins games. Coach your third baseman to try for all balls batted down that way, and have him backed up by the short-stop. Have the second baseman always back up your first baseman, and see that your second baseman and short-stop assist each other.

# A SERMON ON LAWN TENNIS.

### BY JAMES DWIGHT.

LAWN TENNIS is a curious game. It simply consists in hitting a ball over a net and back again. Nothing else, except that you try to hit it as hard as you safely can, and to put it out of your opponent's reach. It sounds easy enough, and yet think how few can play well. You see people play for years, and play very little better at the end. This would be right and natural enough if they took no real interest in the game, but many of them do.

In other games and sports it is not so. There seems to be no game that so many play and so few play well. Any ordinary man can learn to row, respectably at least, if he gives several years to it. Almost any boy can learn to play base-ball. Most men with practice can learn to shoot pretty straight. And so on; but with lawn tennis it is different.

There the multitude are "duffers;" and "duffers" they remain all their lives. It is a few only who come forward out of the ranks.

Why should this be so? For many reasons; the game is not as easy as it looks. It is easy enough to hit the ball gently out of your hand over the net into some part of the opposite court, but it is not so easy to hit it hard and keep it in court. It has to go very close to the net to do that. Then again, it is not enough to hit it into any part of the court; it must be placed in some particular spot to gain any advantage. It may be necessary to place it within a few inches of the side line. On top of all this, you may have to run at the top of your speed to reach the ball at all.

All this does not sound so easy. Yet there is something more, the faculty of playing the right stroke every time. It comes to a very few men as an instinct. It comes to a larger number as the result of years of thought and practice. To the immense majority it never comes at all; in fact, they do not know that such a faculty exists. Even now we have not got through with the difficulties of the game. Running about the court is not easy work. The distance of each man is not great, nor need the speed always be high; but you must start very quickly, almost, in fact, before you are sure where the ball is coming. It is really a succession of jumps, rather than a steady run. For this you need great quickness and agility, and, beyond all, great endurance. In other words, the game needs young men in good condition to play it well. On the other hand, it requires judgment and experience that usually come only later in life.

Such are some of the difficulties of the game; and one does not wonder, as he thinks of them, that the game is not better played. Why, then, some one will ask, is the game so popular? Why do so many play it, if they know that they can never play it well? Because the "duffers" have just as good a time as the "cracks." Sometimes I think that they have a better time even, for with them it is all play; with the better players it is serious work.

I remember well the first time I ever played the game. It was at Nahant, in the summer of '74. A set of lawn tennis had been brought over from England early in the summer; but we had taken no interest in it — too little, indeed, to try it. At length one day we put up the net, marked out a rude court, and started, more in jest than earnest.

In a few moments we were playing in earnest indeed. There was all the feeling of personal antagonism which is to me one of the great attractions of the game. My first opponent was Mr. F. R. Sears, an elder brother of the ex-champion. I remember that each won a game; and that in the afternoon we played in the rain in rubber coats and boots. How odd it would look now!

Of course we could not play much, but the interest was just as great. I fancy that one reason for the great popularity of the game lies in

Playing the Right Stroke.

the fact that you do not need to play well to have a good time. You need only an opponent of about your own strength, so that there may be a continual struggle for the mastery. For this very reason, two players are apt to get into the habit of always playing together, and they naturally improve very slowly. Often they see no good play, they have the same ideas about the game as when they started, they have the same faults, because they know no better.

I look to see much better lawn tennis in the future than exists at present. The game has been generally known about a dozen years; and it was first taken up largely by grown men, who had played rackets, or base-ball, or cricket. They learned all they could with no one to teach them, comparatively soon, and before this time have dropped out of active play because the exertion is beyond them. I am an example of the class myself; though I lasted longer than most, as I cared more for the game.

Of course all this time boys were learning to play, but very few of them turned out well. They learned as they chose; few of them wished for any teaching; fewer got it. So for a long time the older men were in front.

There has now come another change, and in the right direction. The interest in games of all kinds has increased so much, and so much attention is devoted to training boys in the preparatory schools and afterward in college, that we have not only a very large class of trained athletes, but boys have learned how important good "coaching" is. They go into the game more earnestly than they used. Owing to the large number of tournaments, they see the best players, and they copy their styles. Each has some one whom he looks up to as a model of what good play should be.

Now, too, they play in tournaments themselves; and playing in public, they are more careful as to their

*With no Side Twist.*

faults and peculiarities than they used to be in private, for fear of seeming ridiculous. In this way they learn to play well at an earlier age than any class before them. Thus they have their agility and their knowledge of the game at the same time. Heretofore I used to say that the trouble with the game was, that few had brains enough to play it properly until they got too old to play it at all.

This, I think, is no longer true; and the change is due to the improvement of the boys. For instance, I do not see any great improvement in the best players in the past few years, but among the middle-class players the improvement is enormous. They are largely young players, and are still improving. The number, too, of good players has increased very much; and in the first class itself there are twice as many players as there were a few years ago.

The practical part of all this discussion is, "Can we do anything to help the advancement of young players?" Something we can do: we can encourage tournaments between the different schools, etc. The interscholastic tournaments held at Harvard, Yale, and Princeton are good examples. If any one doubts the value of this system, let him look at the success of the foot-ball competition between the different preparatory schools in training players for Harvard. Harvard has not won with them, but that is a different story.

By giving tournaments, we help the boys in several ways. They get used to matches, a very necessary thing. They get interested in the game, and their ambition is aroused. They see good play

A Well-Matched Game.

and good players; and they meet every variety of style, instead of having their practice confined to playing against one or two players only.

This is surely good. Can we now add any preaching that can be of use? I hardly know; I look on preaching with great disrespect. Few listen, few believe you, and fewer still take the trouble to try to put the teaching into practice. There are, however, some general instructions so simple that it would seem folly to write them, if it were not that they are constantly lost sight of.

Take a boy at the beginning. Probably he cannot get one of the most expensive rackets. It really does not matter. Some of the cheaper ones are practically as good, but it matters a great deal what sort of a cheap one he gets. Let him get one of fourteen or fourteen and a quarter ounces, a little lighter in the head than most rackets are made. Have nothing fancy about it, no gold braid, no curious stringing, no fluted handle. It needs to be well balanced and well strung, and that is enough. As to flannels and shoes, there is nothing to be said, except that the shoe should be comfortable and solid enough to hold the foot together, else there is a good deal of danger of straining the foot.

As to balls, I do not know what to say. Balls are very expensive, and last a very short time. A boy cannot expect to have new balls every day; and if he is in earnest, and does not mind taking trouble in order to learn, the best thing that he can do is to practise with two or three balls only. They will need a good deal of chasing, but he will always have them in good condition. If he brings out a boxful, they will all suffer more or less the first day, and he will have to use poor balls till he can get another box. It is a great mistake to use uncovered balls or last year's balls. Neither are of the slightest use.

No advice can be given about courts. One must play on the best available.

To begin with, the player may make up his mind that it will take a long time to play even tolerably well. The first thing to do is to learn to hit the ball straight—that is, with no side twist. The ball should go directly down the court. If the player stands on the central line, the ball should drop on the central line on the other side of the net. This is the very essence of a good stroke.

If you can play straight, you can tell where the ball is going. If you have a curve on it, you will be constantly hitting out of court on the side, or else bringing the ball into the middle of the court when you intended it to go down the side line.

Next in importance is the length of the court. You must learn to hit from one base line to the other; that is, to hit from the back of your own court and make the ball drop about a yard from the other base line. A moment's thought will show that if the ball goes only as far as the service line, your opponent can easily come forward to volley.

A Girl "Champion."

These two points are the foundation of the game.

As to the service, don't bother about it. A very fast service is terrible to bad players; but good ones return it easily. Wait till you play fairly well before you try for a very fast service. Next comes the volley. Wait till you have brought the ground strokes

"A Rest in the Game."

under control before you begin to practise much volleying. When you do begin, keep one point clearly in mind: you must always hit the ball. You must not let it hit your racket. The only exception is when you are close to the net; then you may block the ball, if your opponent is far back. Don't try any wild "smashing." Hit quietly, but always hard. As a principle, never hit a ball easy; always make a real stroke. One word more. Don't play very long at a time. Three or four sets are enough. Always play with a better player if you can, and take odds enough to make him work as hard as he can.

Win quietly; lose quietly, and don't get angry.

## HOW TO TRAIN A CREW.

### BY WILLIAM A. BANCROFT,
*Captain of the Harvard Crews of 1876 to 1879.*

BEFORE training comes the selection of men. Too great care cannot be taken that the members of a crew are, first, physically sound; and, second, anatomically fitted for rowing. Men whose organs are unsound, not only are likely to suffer themselves, but, when they break down, new men are taken in their places, and there is lost the unison of a crew — the result of weeks of preparation. The work must be done over, if there is time. If not, the crew is weakened to that extent. Men should have a suitable stature and suitable proportions. Men too tall or too short, men with extremely long or short arms or legs, conform only with great difficulty, if at all, to the movements of the rest of the crew. Men from five feet eight inches to six feet in height, and weighing, without clothing, from one hundred and fifty to one hundred and eighty-five pounds when in racing condition, are generally the best. There is, of course, great choice in fibre. Some consideration also should be given to temperament and disposition. A man should have resolution, spirit, good judgment, amiability, and equanimity. A good crew must be essentially harmonious, and this involves adaptability on the part of all of its members to each other. Boat-racing should not be undertaken, as a rule, by those under seventeen years of age; and it would be safer to begin at eighteen or even nineteen.

"*On the Machine.*"

The sport is a violent one, and is likely to be too exacting for persons in mid-youth. The organs are not then sufficiently powerful; and an arrested development, even if nothing more serious, may result.

Training involves the amounts and kinds of exercise, food and drink, sleep and bathing for the body, besides the occupation of the mind and its discipline.

And first of *exercise:* —

If the persons selected have the time at their disposal, it is always better, before beginning to row, to practise for a week or two several forms of exercise, for the purpose of strengthening certain muscles of the back and legs, as well as the wrist muscles, and to get the heart and lungs accustomed to greater activity. As the crew, which at this time should contain at least two more men than the number of oars to be pulled, must conform to the powers of its weakest member, and as it is not prudent to begin by taking a large amount of exercise, at first not over twenty minutes ought to be spent on gymnasium apparatus and in calisthenic exercises, and not over a mile ought to be covered in walking and running, three-quarters of which should be walking. This exercise ought to be gradually increased until thirty-five or forty minutes are spent in the gymnasium, and a run of a mile and a half at a pace of seven or eight miles an hour is taken.

The gymnasium exercises should consist of work on vertical bars, on wrist weights, to some extent on arm and chest weights, and in doing the military "setting up" exercises, such as are now prescribed for the army of the United States, especially the exercise which consists in lowering and raising the body by bending the legs at the knees, or "squatting." The gymnasium exercises ought to be done by all together at the word of command, both for the sake of acquiring uniformity of movement, and also of acquiring a habit of obedience. A crew is a machine. Its parts must fit each other, and the whole must start and move and stop as directed.

The "Setting-up" Motion.

These gymnasium exercises for the first two or three years of rowing should be kept up daily, until within about six weeks of a race, usually from ten to fifteen minutes being given to them, even after the actual rowing has begun; and the runs should be kept up until nearly as late a date. During the six weeks or thereabouts immediately preceding a race, a smart walk of a mile or more, according to the time available, ought to be substituted for the exercises and the running. For students and those whose vocations are sedentary, it is a good plan to take the walk immediately upon rising, and, while perspiring, follow it with a quick shower or plunge bath, and a rub-down before breakfast. If there is time, instead of this, a longer walk at a less rapid pace may be taken during the day. Overdoing, however, is to be avoided. What a given crew can do must be learned by experience; and individuals should be relieved, if it is found that they are doing too much. Especially as the day of the race approaches, care should be taken that no one is overtrained. If there is doubt, a given exercise had best be omitted.

The food should consist of meat and fish, vegetables, light puddings, and fruit; the drink of pure water, and good milk if wanted. Pastry, confections, alcoholic drinks, and tobacco should be prohibited. The food should be abundant and wholesome. Steaks, chops, or broiled chicken, with fish for breakfast; soup, fish, and a roast for dinner

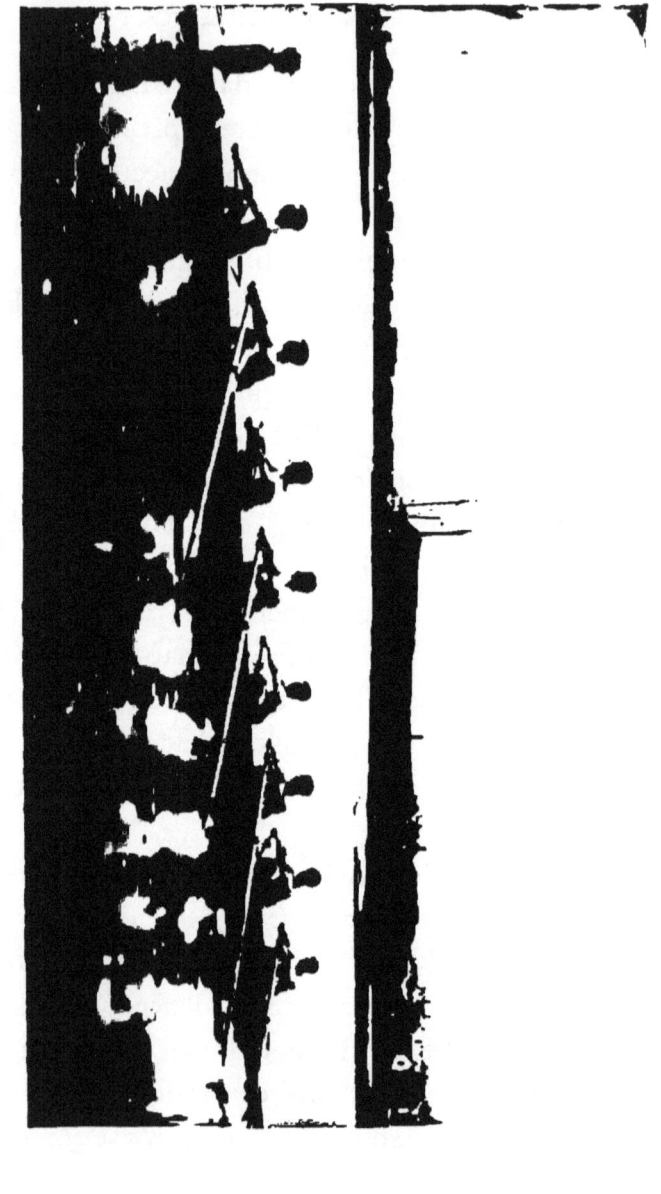

The 'Varsity Crew.
(By permission of Pach Bros., New York, Cambridge, and New Haven.)

in the middle of the day; and a cold roast or breakfast dishes for supper. The roasts should not be overdone, but should be suitably cooked so as to retain the juices. The best of vegetables should be selected, and fruit in its season. The bread should be neither too fresh nor too stale. In short, all these articles of food should be prepared as they are at a first-class hotel. The best of good, wholesome food, and that in abundance, is needed. There ought to be no regret if weight is not lost, provided each man does his share of the work in the boat. Good food and plenty of exercise strengthen the muscles; and if this process is going on, an increase in weight is of little moment.

The oarsman should have all the sleep he wants; and between the ages of eighteen and twenty-five he will need about nine hours in bed, if he does honest work in the boat. He should sleep in a well-ventilated room, and on a hair mattress and pillow, with no more covering than is necessary for warmth, and this will not be much. His sleep should be taken at regular hours. Besides the morning bath, one other cold bath daily may be taken after the row, or after the harder row if there are two; but the bath must be taken while perspiration is going on, that is, at once after the row is done. The bath should not be prolonged, and should be followed by a vigorous rubbing down with a dry towel. This rubbing may advantageously be followed by another rubbing of the limbs by the hands of an attendant, whose hands are moistened with spirits for the purpose. Care, however, should be taken to do the rubbing in a room sufficiently warm and free from draughts to avoid taking cold. If, for any reason, the oarsman has stopped perspiring before taking a bath, the bath should be in warm water.

The mind should have a rational occupation. Freedom from extraordinary care or unusual excitement should be insured. Regularity of both bodily and mental habits should be observed. While in the boat the closest attention should be given by each man to his performance, and time enough should be taken when out of the boat to understand and to master what is required of him. If there is time, and the sole object in view is to win a race, much time may profitably be spent by every member of the crew in perfecting, by discussion or otherwise, the details of the stroke, or of the work of individuals, or of the crew as a whole. At all events, the mind should be kept healthy by the contemplation and the consideration of none but wholesome subjects.

While there should be a regularity in matters of food, sleep, and habits, and, in general, in exercise, the latter should not be allowed to become irksome through its monotony. It is better to give up rowing occasionally for a day, and substitute some other exercise of a recreative character, or rest altogether; and, if the preparation for a race lasts for six months, a vacation of a week ought to be taken when the time is half gone. But even then exercise ought not to be wholly abandoned; and the rest of the requirements, those relating to food, drink, sleep, etc., should be observed.

Few races ought to be undertaken, and none by new men, without at least three months of preparation. By this is not meant that, after a race is over, a man's habits may be radically changed. The true oarsman never essentially changes his habits. Unless his concerns prevent, he will always get plenty of sleep at regular hours, will eat nothing but the kinds of food described above, will not become a slave to any appetite, and will not give up athletic exercise. Such a man will be, in a sense, always in condition; without inconvenience, he will readily assume the more exacting obligations necessary to prepare for a race. A crew of such men may, of course, prepare for a contest in less than three months' time; but even they will do well to give as long a period as three months, if the race is to be any but a very short one.

Position of "Stroke."

The stroke to be rowed will depend somewhat upon circumstances. If it should happen that there be available for the stroke oarsman of the crew, a man who has already acquired a smooth, symmetrical, regular, and effective movement, it may be expedient to teach the rest of the crew his stroke, no matter what the style. Good results have been obtained from such a course. Good crew shell-rowing, no matter what the style of stroke, has certain requirements. The shell must be rowed so that it will not roll from side to side; so that it will not sink unnecessarily either at bow or stern, when the weight of the crew shifts as it is moved with the seats. The oar-blades must take the water on the "full reach" at the very farthest point to which they are carried, without "clipping" or rowing the first part of the stroke in the air. They must take the water also without "backing" it, or throwing it towards the bow. They must leave the water at the end of the stroke without "slivering," or pulling water up as they are taken out; that is, the blades must take and leave the water so that the least possible retardation shall be given to the onward movement of the boat, or, as it is sometimes said, they must be put in and taken out "clean" and "smooth."

After the blades are taken out of the water at the end of the stroke, they must be returned to the "full reach" again without touching the water; for the friction of dragging them along the surface tends to hold the boat back. The blades, of course, ought to be dipped together, taken out together, feathered together at a uniform height, and turned again together for another stroke. Again, there should be uniformity of movement inside the boat; indeed, unless there is such uniformity, there is little likelihood of uniformity of movement outside. The backs, therefore, of a crew that rows well will always be parallel, the legs will move simultaneously, and so will the seats, and the arms will be drawn in at the same time, the wrists dropped together at the finish of the stroke, the arms extended again at the same time, and the hands will be turned simultaneously on the full reach to begin the stroke. All these requirements are common to good crew shell-rowing, and, when lacking, are indications of a faulty stroke. But none of these faults, however, may belong to any one of several crews, no two of which are rowing the same stroke. There may be good rowing, therefore, under various styles of stroke. Still, some one must be adopted.

When no other stroke has been adopted, the following may be used: Assuming the boat to be stationary and the oarsman to be at a " full reach," arms extended, back straightened from its lowest extremity and inclined, seat as far aft as it is intended to be moved, blade in the water turned for the stroke and just covered, the shoulders squared and held down and back, the neck and head in prolongation of the back, the wrist of the hand next to the rowlock slightly convexed, and that hand resting diagonally upon the oar handle, the legs opened slightly, but symmetrically, enough to receive between the thighs the lower front part of the trunk, and the boat resting evenly upon the water, the stroke is begun by swaying the trunk back as though pivoted at the seat until it has reached the vertical position, then the legs are straightened out with vigor, the seat moving back with the shoulders, the hands being kept at such a height that the blade will remain just covered, until the seat has been moved toward the bow to its limit, and the trunk has swung just a trifle beyond the vertical. The stroke is finished by drawing in the arms until the hands touch the body, when, by dropping them a bit, and, at the same time slightly turning the wrist, the blade is taken out of the water. Care should be taken to keep the blade just covered in making this finish. To return to the "full reach" again the hands continue moving, and are shot out parallel with the surface of the water until the arms are straightened, the trunk is swung forward, and almost

*In Single Scull.*

at the same time the seat is started aft, while the trunk continues to swing until everything gets to the "full reach" simultaneously and is ready to begin another stroke. Nothing but practice, of course, and the assistance of an experienced "coach," will enable a crew to row smoothly, gracefully, and effectively the stroke here attempted to be described. The separate parts of the stroke are given as though they were independent movements, instead of forming, as they do, one continuous but complicated movement. At the beginning of the stroke, or at the "catch" as it is called, the shoulders should be driven back vigorously and rapidly, care being taken not to make the motion a jerky one by burying the oar-blade too deeply, and thus stopping the movement of the shoulders. At the finish the most difficult part of the movement to be acquired is a rapid "shoot" of the arms away from the body, without a jarring motion by which the hands are either sent down into the lap with a violent thump, or else the shoulders are brought forward with a jerk. The "catch" and the "shoot" give no little trouble to beginners; but, when once mastered by a crew, it is believed that, other things being equal, no stroke without them is so effective. Every motion must be such as to waste no energy. After the arms are shot out, the trunk, which scarcely stops in changing direction, should not be rushed towards the "full reach," but should follow at a relatively moderate pace the "shoot" of the arms. Especially, care should be taken not to let the trunk drop down on the "full reach" with a jar or thump, and pains should be taken to have the hands high enough as they approach the "full reach" to bring the blade as close to the water as it can be brought, without "backing water," to begin the stroke.

The tricks of watermanship, or of rowing the boat "on an even keel" as it is called, that is,

*A Turn to Starboard.*

without its inclining either to port or starboard, can most of them be learned only by experience. It is a general rule, when the boat inclines to port during the feather, for the starboard men to lower their hands and for the port men to raise theirs, and *vice versâ*. If the boat rolls to port during the stroke, the port men must pry her over, done by lifting, as it were, their oar-handles, and *vice versâ*. Every muscle should, of course, be trained to be under absolute control, so as to adjust itself to the various conditions of wind, wave, and current as they appear, to anticipate, and, by the necessary motions, to counteract their effect upon the "trim" of the boat. Power must be applied vigorously at one instant; at the next, it must be taken off so as to maintain the "beat" or rhythm of the stroke.

It is best to teach a novice the motions of the trunk, legs, and arms upon a rowing-machine. The muscles are then accustomed to many of the requirements of the stroke, so that when, later, the beginner is seated in a boat, there is not so much to be learned at once. Before he is allowed to row with a crew, he should be taught first, in a pair-oared boat of sufficient steadiness not to roll, the proper method of handling an oar. From the pair-oar, the members of the crew should next be seated in a steady barge, and there be taught to row "together." Lastly, the shell should be entered. In the meantime, the way to lift boats, to carry them, to put them into the water and to take them out should be taught; also the way to get in and to get out of a boat; the way to turn a boat without straining it, as well as how to "hold" it and to "back" it. A shell must be used with the greatest of care, in order that its lines may be kept.

In placing the crew in a boat, care should be taken to select for the stroke oarsman a man of quick motions, clear head, and self-possession, plucky, and of endurance. He should be able to set a long stroke, the pace of which he can regulate without throwing the crew out of time, and he should have power enough to "drive" the rest of the crew in a spurt. The next man behind the stroke oarsman should be a stronger man than he, and one who rows a stroke quite as long, and who can keep in perfect time with him. The weight of the crew should be so arranged that the boat will never "trim down by the head," that is, sink lower in the bow than in the stern; and, as nearly as possible, the strength of the men on one side should equal the strength of those on the other.

There are two objects in training a crew —

one to enable it to acquire an effective stroke, the other to enable its members to be in the very best physical condition at the hour of the race. The first consideration should always yield to the second.

# CRICKET AS PLAYED IN AMERICA.

### BY RALPH CRACKNELL.
*Of the Boston Athletic Association and Longwood Cricket Club.*

ENGLISH and American boys are pretty much the same kind of fellows in their love of outdoor sports; and in neither country does a boy get into knickerbockers, without beginning at once to learn to play ball.

The very small boy is usually content to begin by playing "catch;" that is, tossing the ball back and forth; but it is only a short time before we find him trying to follow the example of the older boys, and play the national game — in America, base-ball; in England, cricket.

And as soon as he becomes a pretty fair player, we find our boy joining some small club; next, playing on his school team; then on his college nine or eleven, and all the while going to see games between the best players of the great teams, studying the fine points of the game, learning the science of play, and unconsciously getting the good health which comes from being in the open air, and which is likely to carry him through life.

The difference between the games of the two countries, is, however, that cricket means much more to the English boy than base-ball does to the American.

This follows naturally; for while our American game has been in existence only about thirty-five years, cricket has been the English national sport for two centuries; and where, with us, our best players of base-ball are men who make a business of playing, and are paid large salaries, in England the greatest cricket teams are made up very largely of amateurs, it being seldom that in one game more than two or three professional players will be found.

It is this strictly amateur element of the game of cricket that has won, and kept for it, its popularity in England, where the hero of the hour in school, college, county, and international matches is the one who has made a big score, or broken through the defence of his opponents by skilful bowling.

Many boys will be surprised to learn that the first game of cricket played in America, of which we have record, was between eleven colonists and an equal number of Londoners, in 1751, and we take pleasure in recording the fact that the "cockneys" were beaten.

In Boston, in 1809, the first organized club was started by a number of Englishmen, under the name of the Boston Cricket Club; and just twenty-one years afterward the St. George's Club, of New York, was founded, and began the work of fostering and encouraging the progress of the game.

Cricket is so little understood by the many to whom base-ball and tennis have been the principal summer sports, that it may be well to give a brief outline of its objects, and the way it is played.

A field as large as possible, in which the grass is kept as carefully clipped and level as a lawn, is the ideal cricket ground. Near the centre of the field, the pitch, as it is called, is selected, and the wickets are placed twenty-two yards apart, opposite and parallel to each other.

It must be understood that the "pitch" alluded to is the space which corresponds to the space between the pitcher and catcher in base-ball.

Each wicket consists of three round wooden sticks, called "stumps," which are driven into the ground, and just near enough together to prevent the ball from passing between them, while their height must not exceed twenty-seven inches, and their total width, when ready for attack, not more than eight inches.

On top of each wicket are placed two small sticks of wood, called "bails;" and so lightly are they poised that at the slightest disturbance of the wicket they fall to the ground.

*Ready for the Attack.*

The bowler's crease, corresponding in base-ball to the pitcher's box, from behind which the ball must be bowled, is in line with the wicket. Another line, four feet from the wicket and parallel with it, is called the popping crease; and the batsman, to be safe, must have some part of his body or his bat inside this line when the ball is in play.

The bat used is made of willow, with a spliced handle, usually of cane. It is nearly flat, and not more than four and a quarter inches wide, or more than thirty-eight inches long. The ball has a basis of cork, and is bound with leather, and weighs between five and one-half and five and three-quarters ounces.

A match is played between two sides, of eleven players each, unless otherwise agreed; each side has two innings except in one-day matches, when one innings each decides the contest.

The chance of innings is decided by tossing. The batting side sends two men to the wickets, and, as each man gets out, another replaces him until the whole side is out; one man being "not out," because by the rules of the game there must be a batsman at each wicket.

The side which takes the field selects two bowlers, one of whom delivers four, five, or six balls as previously arranged.

The umpire, at the bowler's wicket, now calls, "over." The field then changes to suit the bowler from the opposite end, and he delivers the same number of balls, when "over" is called by the other umpire, and the field changes again, and so on.

The bowler's object is to hit the wicket; or he is to bowl such a ball that the batsman hits it in the air, and is caught by a fielder, or is coaxed outside of the popping crease, when, missing the ball, the wicket is knocked down by the wicket keeper, who corresponds to the catcher in base-ball, and the batsman is stumped out.

The batsman's object is to hit the ball through the fielders, or in such a location as to give no chance for a catch, and score a run. A run is

"*How's that?*"—*Stumped Out.*

scored as often as the batsmen, after a hit, or at any time while the ball is in play, shall have crossed, and made good their ground, from end to end. If caught between the wickets while running, or if at any time the batsman while in play is out of his ground, and his wicket be struck down by the ball after touching any fieldsman, he is "run out."

With a few minor rules added, this is the way

in which the game is played in England and America.

The placing of the field, which is done by the bowler or the captain of the team, requires the greatest judgment, so that the kind of ball delivered receives the support it should by the fielders when hit by the batsman. The field can be changed at any time during an "over."

The difference between bowling and pitching is that the ball must not be thrown.

The arm must be straight as it leaves the shoulder. The bowler twists and curves the ball from the ground. The pitcher makes his curves, and shoots in the air.

Returning to the history of cricket in America, we find that in 1855, with the formation of the Young America Club in Philadelphia, the game began to acquire an American individuality which has since marked the play of the followers of the game in the Quaker City,—the leading cricket city in America. It has been called the "home of American cricket." Through the influence of the cricketers of that city, teams from England, Ireland, and Australia have visited this country; and each contest has marked the progress of the game in America, until, in 1891, the Philadelphians gained a brilliant victory over a strong eleven of English cricketers, captained by Lord Hawke.  A few years ago an eleven of university men from Ireland visited this country, and won one match with Philadelphia, and lost one, drawing a third.  The Philadelphians, however, did not play in their best form, and probably underrated their opponents, who had suffered defeat in Boston when playing twelve men against fifteen.

At matches like those last mentioned, the attendance at the beautiful Manheim grounds of the Germantown Cricket Club, where the international contests are played, rivals that of an important match in England or Australia.  In England the largest attendance on record is at a match played last season between Surrey and Nottinghamshire, when, in the three days, seventy-eight thousand people passed through the gates.  In Australia the record was made in a match between England and Australia, when sixty thousand people attended.  At Manheim, during the three days' match with Lord Hawke's eleven, over twenty-five thousand people visited the grounds; and the scene was as picturesque and as animated as can be witnessed at Lords

*An International Cricket Match.*

when a university match, or the crack public school match between Eton and Harrow, is being played.

The patron or player of base-ball, accustomed to the bare-looking field, with its tawdry grand stand, and rows of uncomfortable wooden seats called "bleachers," would be agreeably surprised could he see the beauty and luxury which surround the game of cricket as played at Manheim.

*Bowler Delivering a Ball.*

Skirting the ground, drawn up in the welcome shade of tall, graceful trees, are coaches crowded with ladies in light costumes, many wearing the colors of their favorite elevens. Inside these, and completely surrounding the ground, is a black line of spectators ten and twelve deep, with here and there groups of old cricketers chatting of the past contests, and liberally applauding any good play. In the middle, is the arena where the battle is being fought; the white flannels of the men as they move over the green turf, the constant activity, the call to players, and the shouts of the audience, making a most animated scene. To this, are added the beautiful pavilions, crowded from floor to roof. These include: first, the great main pavilion, used for the members of the club, the players, and their 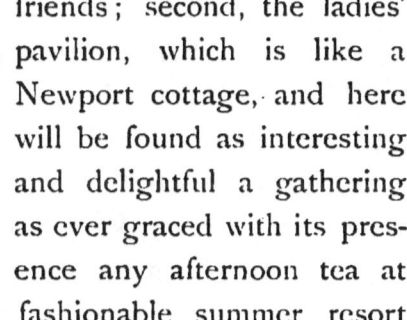 friends; second, the ladies' pavilion, which is like a Newport cottage, and here will be found as interesting and delightful a gathering as ever graced with its presence any afternoon tea at that fashionable summer resort by the sea.

*Blocking a Twist from Leg.*

Last, but by no means least in importance, is the boys' pavilion; and here is one of the chief factors in making cricket in Philadelphia so successful.

Great pains are taken to encourage boys to take up the game. They have this pavilion, and their ownership is marked by the sign of the "kid."

The custom of Philadelphians in training up the youth to love the game of cricket, and to know its fine points, has placed that city in the front rank of the cricket cities in America. Boston has a good club at Longwood, and several Americans play the game there; but cricket in New England is at present played principally by Englishmen. The same is true of New York, Chicago, and Detroit, and partly so of Baltimore and Pittsburg.

Not until the schools and colleges of America take up the game will it become universally understood, and reach the popularity it has attained in other English-speaking countries.

St. Paul's School, near Concord, N. H., has a beautiful cricket ground; and there can be found the same interest, rivalry, and skill, as in a large English school. Haverford College and the University of Pennsylvania have been the educational grounds of many of Philadelphia's famous cricketers. Harvard has struggled manfully to support an eleven, and Yale in some years has attempted to do so, but the interest is very slight.

With its rank as an amateur sport, and its qualities of good nature, courtesy, and forbearance, which are necessary to make a true cricketer, and with its opportunity for exercise after more active games have been given up, cricket should, in America, receive the encouragement it can justly claim.

## GOLF: THE COMING GAME.

### BY HUGH S. HART.
*Of the Xavier Athletic Association.*

GOLF is the coming game. Already it has more than kept pace with its younger rivals; and, from a purely local Scotch game, has extended its fascinations to every English-speaking community.

That the international popularity of golf, widespread as it already is, will go on increasing, seems an assured fact, as it is based on certain unique characteristics, in which the grand old game has no rivals.

In golfing, the mental, as well as the physical and muscular, qualities are called into full play. Like the surface of the ideal golf link, the game presents a series of perpetual changes. Difficulty after difficulty arises, which the player is called upon to surmount by cool judgment and prompt action. The same complication may never occur twice in identical circumstances; therefore the ingenuity, skill, and intelligence of the golfer have unlimited scope.

Meanwhile, although the violent, intermittent exercise, which renders baseball, cricket, and foot-ball impracticable to all save veritable athletes, can always be avoided in golf; the legs and arms are called into equable and invigorating action.

*A Long Stroke.*

Unlike almost all other out-door games, golf can be played all the year round. This is even possible during the winter months, as an admirable game can be insured upon the snow by the use of red balls.

But its most generally appreciated peculiarity is, that it may include among its devotees five of Shakespeare's "Seven ages of man," from the immature schoolboy to the "lean and slippered pantaloon;" while the girls, too, are afforded an equal opportunity to develop practical enthusiasm, if not proficiency.

Almost the only indispensable requisite of a golf course is space. If a sufficient area is available, the impracticability of the surface for other games is rather a recommendation ; all such irregularities and impediments are known as "bunkers." Without these, all would be literally flat, stale, and unprofitable to the chronic golfer, who estimates his enjoyment by the number of "hazards" such obstructions oblige him to play.

The full course may be any distance from three to five miles, though a course half the size may be played round twice. Eighteen holes, from four and a half to five inches in depth and diameter, are cut in the turf at intervals, not necessarily equidistant, and kept in shape with a metal lining.

The turf around each hole for about twenty yards must be perfectly level. These spaces are known as "putting greens," and are tended as so many gardens. In each hole is placed a long rod, surmounted by a flag, to indicate its locality; but should the course be unusually undulating, additional "guide flags" are placed to mark the route from hole to hole. These flags should be of a uniform color for half the circuit, while those indicating the return route should be a distinct contrast.

Adjoining each "putting green," a small space within painted lines is reserved as a "teeing ground." It is from this the ball is "teed" toward the next hole. To facilitate the game, a box of sand is generally placed within reach of the players; and, from this, a bit of sand may be taken to elevate the ball slightly, and insure a clean and effective hit.

*Among the Bunkers.*

The ball used is of solid rubber, about five inches in circumference. The game commences by each side playing a ball from the teeing ground, where the start and finish of the course converge in the direction of the first hole. A side may consist of one or more players, and two or more sides constitute a game. The hole is won by the side "holing its ball" in the fewest strokes. When the strokes are equal, the hole is divided.

As the hole is approached by the leading player, the flagstaff is temporarily removed until the hole is scored. The ball is then struck from the adjacent "teeing ground" in the direction of the second hole, and so on. In a match the partners strike alternately from the tees, and also during the play of the hole.

The players who are to strike against each other should be named at starting, and continue in the same order. The side winning a hole leads in starting for the next. This privilege is called the "honor."

One round of the links (a round amounts generally to eighteen holes in all) is a match, unless otherwise agreed upon. The match is won by the side which gets more holes ahead than remain to be played, or by the side winning the last hole when the score is even at the previous one.

When there is only one player on each side, the match is called a "singles." Two players on a side constitute a "foursome." These are the two most common and popular forms of golf.

What lends golf the variety and uncertainty which are its chief fascinations, is the diversified surface over which it is played. All obstructions, from scrub to stone walls, intercept the ball in its progress from hole to hole. As it cannot be handled, save in very exceptional cases, it must be "played out" of the "bunker" or "hazard" which stopped its flight. To make the smallest number of strokes to release it, clubs in great variety are used.

A moderate golf equipment is supposed to include the

Teeing with the Driver.

driver, long spoon, short spoon, brassy, driving iron, lofting iron, mashy, cleek, niblick, and putter. The first four and the last have wooden heads. The remainder are of iron. The driver is used for "teeing," and easy, long-distance strokes. The long spoon is used in high grass, and when elevation of the ball is desired. The "driving" and

*On the Putting Green.*

"lofting" irons serve as more powerful alternates. The short spoon is used for short drives, and when the player stands below the level of the ball. The brassy, niblick, and cleek are tried in very awkward "hazards." The "mashy" and "putter" come into play when on or near the "putting green."

# ABOUT BICYCLES.

### BY KIRK MUNROE.
*Founder of the League of American Wheelmen.*

NEVER, since the beginning of the world, have boys and girls been provided with so many opportunities for having good times, combined with healthful recreation, as in these days of what is truly called "the age of sports." Boating and canoeing on the water, tennis and bicycling on land, are as freely offered to girls as to boys, with baseball, la crosse, cricket, and foot-ball, thrown in as extras for the latter. Of all these sports it seems to me that bicycling should rank first, not only for the pleasure that it gives, and the excellent exercise that it affords, but on account of the practical good that the bicycle is accomplishing. One of the chief needs of this great country is good roads. The value of a farm is doubled the moment it is connected with its nearest market town by a well macadamized road. Not only this, but all its products can be sold more cheaply to the dwellers in towns and cities. But very few people realized how bad our American roads were until they began to ride bicycles over them. Then they found out quickly enough; and now every wheelman in the country is an advocate of good roads. This being the case, I am sure that when the great and ever-increasing army of boy and girl riders of to-day become old enough to have a voice in public affairs, their very first demand will be for good roads for their bicycles throughout the length and breadth of the land.

There are many complaints made that bicycles are ridden on sidewalks, and we see signs everywhere forbidding this practice — that is, everywhere in the neighborhood of bad roads; for where the roads are good the signs are not necessary. If the roads were as smooth and hard as the sidewalks, or even smoother and harder, as they should be, no bicycle rider would ever think of taking to the sidewalks, or have the slightest desire to do so. With such roads as the Beacon Street extension running out of Boston, or many that exist in Brookline and the Newtons, or around Chestnut Hill Reservoir, or in Central Park and the New York boulevards, or in the Oranges of New Jersey, or in Fairmount Park of Philadelphia, or Druid Hill Park of Baltimore, or the streets of Washington, or the Chicago boulevards, or the Cliff Drive in San Francisco, no wheelman has any inclination to ride on the sidewalks, nor are any warning signs needed. Where, on the other hand, he comes to such disgraceful, rocky, sandy, and rutty roads as exist in and around most of the smaller cities and towns of the country, he must either give up riding entirely, or else take to the footpaths and sidewalks; and in spite of the risk of arrest and fine thus incurred, he generally prefers to do the latter.

In this connection I wish to suggest to all young bicycle riders that there is no time or place where politeness pays better than when you find yourself compelled by the state of the roads to share a footpath with pedestrians. They have as good a right there as you have — probably a better one. Do not, then, attempt to pass them without warning and at full speed, or shout to them to " look out of the way," or demand a free passage by the ringing of bells or the blowing of shrill whistles. All of these things are rude, startling, and exceedingly ill-bred. Moreover, they serve to make enemies where, it is most important the bicycle should have friends. No one will refuse to allow you room to pass if you slacken speed, and politely ask him to do so; and a pleasant "Thank you" in acknowledgment of the courtesy thus rendered will go far toward securing that person's favorable consideration of the rights of bicycles, and the need of good roads for them, the next time the question is brought to his attention.

Now, boys, for a word with you. Will you tell me why, as a rule, you double yourselves up like jackknives, and bend over so as to almost touch your handle-bars while riding? Is it because you think it a becoming attitude? Well, it isn't. It makes you look like so many wooden monkeys, climbing sticks. If you gain any speed by it you do so at the expense of wind, for it is certain that you can't breathe so well in that position as when sitting straight. Besides, do you find it necessary or even enjoyable to "scorch" or ride at full speed all the time? I will admit that in riding up a steep hill, or against a strong wind, there is something to be gained by bending over, though it is not necessary even in those cases. In horseback riding only jockeys, while engaged in racing, bend low over the horse's neck. The road rider who assumes such a position would be a subject for derision. Moreover, by persistent bending over, you are weakening your lungs, curving your spines, and rounding your shoulders. You are training yourselves to become crooked-backed, hollow-chested, stoop-shouldered men. If this is what the bicycle is doing for you, it would be better that you had never seen one. So there, boys, drop this practice of bending over just as quickly as you know how. Sit up as straight as the girls do, or, better still, as straight as a cavalry soldier on parade; throw back your shoulders, expand your lungs, and in after years you will have good cause to bless the day that gave you your first bicycle.

As for the girl bicycle riders who, as a rule, put the boys to shame by riding as straight as though they were on horseback, I am afraid that in some cases they only do so because they can't bend over and breathe at the same time. How is it, girls? Are not some of you trying to ride in corsets, or at least in tight waists and belts? If so, you are preparing for yourselves a future of even greater suffering and unhappiness than the monkey-like boys who bend low over their handle-bars; and to you,

*A Halt by the Way.*

(*By permission of the Western Wheel Works, Chicago, Ill.*)

too, I would say that it were better never to have seen a bicycle than to attempt to ride under such conditions. Can you, when dressed for a ride, raise your arms straight above your head and bring the palms of your hands together? Can you stoop over and touch your toes with the tips of your fingers without bending the knees? If you can, your riding costume is all right. If you cannot, it is all wrong.

Before dropping the subject of riding costumes, I want to suggest that bicycle riding is a most energetic form of exercise, and that one becomes quickly heated by it even on a cool day; therefore, the wearing of underclothing of light flannel, which readily absorbs perspiration, is most important. In these days of pneumonia and kindred troubles, it is also very desirable that a coat, jacket, or sweater should form part of the equipment of every bicycle. It should be compactly folded, and strapped to the handle-bar or luggage-carrier during the ride, and put on by the rider the moment a halt is called. It makes little difference how thinly you are clad while engaged in the heating exercise of riding, so long as you are provided with a warm over-garment to cool off in. All athletes recognize this necessity.

Note, for instance, the heavy woollen sweaters that are drawn over the heads of the foot-ball men the moment they stop play. We blanket our overheated horses in order to save them from the effects of a too sudden cooling. Shall we not give to ourselves at least the same amount of care that we bestow upon them?

So much for the rider. Now for the machine. The bicycle is at once the lightest, strongest, and most easy-running of all wheeled vehicles. With its air-cushioned rubber tires, steel spokes, ball bearings, spring seat, and hollow steel frame, it is perfectly adapted to its work. At the same time all of its adjustments are so delicate and so dependent upon each other, that a disturbance of any one affects the whole machine. A squeak or rattle should not be tolerated for a minute. Every properly equipped tool-bag contains the means for removing either of these nuisances. Always examine and test every part of your bicycle before starting on a ride, and never fail to have your tool-bag provided with wrench, screw-driver, a full oil-can, a bit of soft rag, and a small bottle of cement. Above all, make a point of knowing your machine, its every adjustment, screw, and nut, as well as you know your alphabet, before you take it away from the place at which you have purchased it.

Do not attempt to ride either far or fast at first. The bicycle brings into play a different set of muscles from any that you have exercised before, and you must give them time to become accustomed to their work. When they have done so, and you have obtained a perfect mastery of your machine, you will be able to take daily rides of from ten to fifty miles with less effort than you formerly expended in walking a third of those distances. To the wheelman, free to go when and where he will, to stop where and for as long as he pleases, to regulate his speed at will, and thus to have absolute control of his own movements, all other modes of conveyance seem tame and inadequate. With all this the bicycle is now among the cheapest of luxuries. Any boy or girl may earn one by obtaining a few new subscribers to some popular or enterprising magazine; while those whose means will permit them to purchase outright will find by consulting the advertisements that prices are tumbling all the time. Twenty years ago I paid more for an old wooden-wheeled, iron-tired, plain bearing, and springless velocipede, or "bone-shaker" as it is now called, than would purchase a first-class safety bicycle to-day. Wherefore, my young readers, be thankful that your youth has come to you in an age of bicycles, rather than in one of "boneshakers."

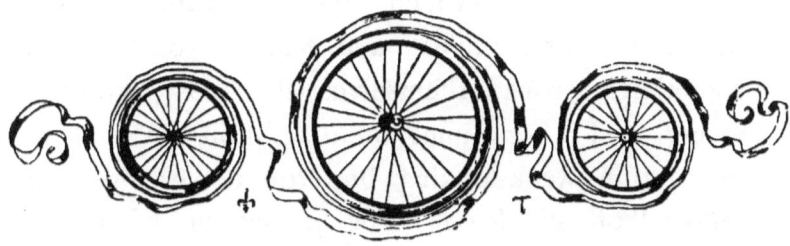

# RUNNING AND HURDLING.

### BY NORMAN W. BINGHAM, JR.
*Captain Harvard Track Team of 1895.*

SCARCELY any form of athletics has so many followers who differ so absolutely in physique from the popularly accepted idea of an "athlete," as do the so-called "pedestrian" sports, which include running and hurdling. The frailest and palest youths have sometimes proved themselves the most powerful racers; and it is no uncommon sight on the track to see a thin, weak-looking boy run a big, muscular fellow "off his feet." The possession of a pair of long legs is no assurance that their owner will be able to get over the ground quickly, nor, as has often been proved, do decidedly short ones prevent his doing so. The fact is, there is absolutely no means of judging off-hand what sort of a racer one will make. For this reason, the boy who is too small to play foot-ball or to row, or was not born with the base-ball instinct in him, may turn his attention to the cinder-path, with the consoling thought that from just such as he many a champion has been developed.

There is no better athletic sport than running; none which should bring with it less danger of physical injury, and none which demands so small an amount of time daily for practice, or getting into "form." Lasting and serious harm, however, may result from improper training.

The boy who desires to enter for a foot-race should, first of all, be sure that his heart is strong; he should assure himself that he has no special weakness which the strain of competition might aggravate.

He probably knows whether his abilities lie in the direction of long or short distances. Only actual trials and racing experience, however, can determine for just what distance he is best fitted. There are often cases in which boys start out with the idea of going into the short dashes, and, after attaining little success at that, turn out first-class middle-distance or distance runners. A poor showing in a first race, then, should not discourage a boy from further effort.

The most popular distances with amateurs in America are the one hundred yards' dash, the two hundred and twenty yards' dash, quarter-mile, half-mile, and mile runs. The three-mile and five-mile runs are less often attempted, and the still longer distances are seldom covered except in "cross-country" running.

There are many theories as to the best method of preparing for each one of these distances. One trainer may tell you to do one thing, and another will say that is just wrong. Moreover, persons of different temperaments and dispositions will not always do well under the same treatment. Experience alone will prove just how much and what sort of work will bring a man into the best possible condition. Without attempting to discuss or compare the advantages of different training methods, I shall simply attempt to throw out a few hints to boys who have no chance to secure a trainer, or to watch others train.

The first danger to be avoided is that of trying to do too much at once. I shall always remember one evening on Holmes' Field in Cambridge, watching a number of "town" boys training. Some were tearing wildly about the track as if running for a record; others had thrown themselves on the grass exhausted.

A young man with a stop-watch in his hand called out to a very weary-looking lad who had thrown himself face-downward on the grass: —

"Let's see, Jo, what you training for?"

"Quarter," was the reply.

"What ye done to-night?"

"Jogged two miles."

"Feel like being timed a quarter?"

"Well, I reckon I'll run one first, 'n' see how m' wind is."

So up jumped the sprinter; he ran around the track at a smart pace, and then ran his quarter-mile on time.

Absurd as it seemed, it was but the exaggeration of the common fault of all beginners — a tendency to do more than is good for them.

If the beginner intends to "sprint" — that is, run the short distances up to a quarter-mile — he had better, for a few days, take slow jogs of three hundred or four hundred yards.

Having accustomed his muscles to the exercise, he may vary this work every other day by running at fair speed for about two-thirds of the distance he intends to made his specialty. If it be the hundred-yard dash, he may do it twice, with a few minutes' rest between each dash. The slow work will serve to strengthen the muscles, and the quick work to keep them limber. Proceeding in this manner, the sprinter should be able, after ten days or two weeks, to run at top speed without danger of straining his muscles.

The Standing Start.

So much depends on a good start in sprint races that much of a man's time must be devoted to getting away quickly after the starter's pistol is fired.

In all races the starter gives two preliminary commands to the men before sending them off. At the first — "On your marks!" — the men are supposed to take their positions on the track; they may, if they like, scrape out small holes to prevent the feet from slipping in starting. Then the word comes, "Set!" when the contestants get in position, ready for the signal "Go." As every false start entails the penalty of being set back, it is necessary that this position should be a steady one.

Speaking generally, there are two prominent styles of starting, each of which, however, has its modifications.

First, there is the standing start, which is used by all long-distance runners when there is no need of starting off in the lead. The runner plants one foot on the "scratch," or starting-line, the other foot is placed from twenty inches to a yard back; then throwing the weight as far forward as is possible without losing the balance, with one arm thrust forward and the other back, he is "set."

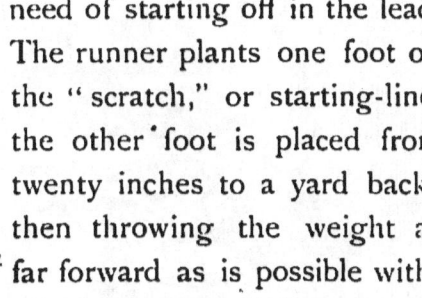
The Low or "Crouching" Start.

Nearly all sprinters nowadays, however, have adopted some form of the low or "crouching" start. The commonest and perhaps the easiest way to learn is that in which both feet are back of "scratch." One foot is planted a few inches behind the line, and the other from six inches to a foot still farther back. When told to set, the run-

*A Close Finish.*

ner stoops, places his hands or finger-tips on the mark, and throws his weight forward on the arms. When the hands are raised from the ground the tendency is to pitch forward, and he must either run or fall. A start which is used successfully by many sprinters is a sort of combination between a standing and crouching position. The runner takes his position as if for a standing start, with his feet spread a trifle farther apart. At the word " set," he places the hand corresponding to the forward foot on the line just inside that foot, and thus divides his weight between the arm and leg. This affords him the advantage of being steadier than in the standing start, and does not give him so much of a strain as does the low start. Of course, on the days that are devoted to starting, the runner can make his other work lighter. It is well, also, while starting, to keep on occasionally and run out for forty or fifty yards. Otherwise it may be difficult for a man to get into his regular stride after he starts.

The general scheme of training for the sprints may, to speak very roughly, be applied to the other distances. That is to say, there must be some long work, and more shorter fast work. As I have said before, however, no two men can train in exactly the same manner. Delicate men who rely largely on their "nerve" to carry them through a race, cannot stand as much severe work as their more rugged fellows, though they may run their races quite as fast.

Men who are training for distances from the quarter mile up scarcely need to be sent beyond their distance oftener than once or twice a week. The rest of the time may be spent in running from half to two-thirds the distance at a much sharper pace.

As to a man's "style" in running, there is not much to be said, except that he should be as natural as possible. He should stride out freely, getting his knees well up in front of him, but should not attempt to step too far. The arms should swing easily backward and forward, and should not be hugged up to the chest in such a way as to contract the lungs. Above all, don't attempt to run with your mouth closed. It is pitiful to see some men half strangle themselves in a race by attempting to breathe through the nose alone.

"Hurdling" (or leaping over obstructions while running) requires not only the speed and endurance of flat-running, but also a coolness and grace which some men can never acquire.

There is a material difference between hurdling and a common jump. The spring being taken from one foot, the other should be brought up so that it will be nearly as high as the knee, and only slightly forward of it.

The leg from which the spring is taken should be allowed to follow with the foot well back, and knee up to one side. Never hurry this foot forward. In order to clear the hurdles with the smallest possible loss of time, the athlete must regulate his stride so as to be ready to leave the ground at practically the same distance from each hurdle. He must not go higher than is absolutely necessary to clear the hurdles, and must land on the ground poised in a position to continue his running.

The two popular distances with hurdlers are one hundred and twenty yards, and two hundred and twenty yards. In the former, there are ten hurdles, usually three feet six inches in height, and placed ten yards apart. The first hurdle is fifteen yards from the scratch. In this race the runner is able to get in just three strides between the hurdles. This forces him to take his spring, every time, from the same foot. Fear of the hurdles, and a tendency to get too near them before leaving the ground, are difficulties against which the beginner has to contend. If his stride comes right, however, and he is able to run fast between the hurdles, it will only require practice to enable him to run through with as much certainty about coming up to the hurdles properly as if he were a machine. One well-known high hurdler has expressed confidence in his ability to run his race blindfolded.

The two hundred and twenty yard hurdles are each two feet six inches high, placed twenty yards apart, the first one being set twenty yards from the start. The runner will find it necessary to take either seven, eight, or nine strides between the hurdles. The best hurdlers require only seven. This enables the runner to spring or "take off" always with the same foot. Few men, however, have a long enough stride or sufficient endurance to enable them to go through all ten hurdles, taking only seven strides between. Eight strides demand of the runner the ability to "take off" equally well with either foot, while nine strides are too many to enable a man to attain any great speed between hurdles. The ability to hurdle easily may be gained in the winter by using a single hurdle in the gymnasium.

Leaping the Hurdles.

Whether in flat-running or hurdling, it should always be remembered that a race is won at the finish. There the supreme effort should be made. It is a frequent mistake with novices to stop running a yard or two from the finish, and many a race has been lost in this way.

Chapters might be written about the proper way to run the different distances, but the fine points of racing are best learned from experience.

# HARE AND HOUNDS RUNS.

BY DAVID W. FENTON, 2D.
*Harvard and Manhattan Cross-Country Teams, 1892.*

LONG before cinder tracks and spiked shoes were known, our ancestors settled their disputes of superiority in regard to their powers of speed by running across the meadows and plains. It is an interesting fact to note the decline of this long-distance running during the past century, and its revival again, chiefly through the medium of hare and hounds runs, in the larger American universities.

Any one who has enjoyed these runs on brisk fall afternoons, and experienced their invigorating effects, will never avoid an opportunity to take part in this popular out-door sport. The delicate youth who is urged into it by the enthusiasm of the old runners, increases his powers of endurance, gains health and strength, and sees Nature in all her beauty.

The general code of rules governing hare and hounds runs, often called "paper chases," is practically the same in all the larger colleges. Two of the runners, termed hares, start out in ordinary running costume with canvas bags filled with paper cut in pieces an inch square. The paper,

*A Hare. — Scattering Scent.*

or "scent," is scattered profusely along the course, so that it may be easily followed. Five minutes later, the pack of hounds break away, headed by the master of hounds, whose duties are to set the pace and keep the men together. The trail must be followed at all times except where there is water, in which case the runners can go around the stream or ford it, as they choose. The hares run much faster than the hounds, as the former must make up a time allowance of seven minutes; that is, the hares must arrive at the starting-point twelve minutes before the arrival of the first hound, or else they are caught. After the hares have run in a circuitous route, ranging from five to

*The Hares. — Coming to the Break.*

ten miles, they strew a profusion of paper on the ground as the signal for the "break." When the hounds reach this point, they line up, wait awhile for the stragglers, and then break away, racing for home. The first and second hounds in at the finish receive appropriate prizes.

The hares are rarely caught, as many circumstances cause much loss of time by the hounds. Sometimes the wind blows away part of the scent, and the small boys along the route often pick up the bits of paper and lay a false trail. Thus much time may be lost in discovering the true course. The desire for prizes has sometimes caused the hares to lay double trails and resort to other unsportsmanlike means to deceive the hounds; but this fault has been remedied by the passage of a rule which provides that the hares shall receive no prizes.

The ideal course usually lies about a hilly country, through patches of woods, and over fences with numerous water-jumps occurring along the way. These different obstacles lend variety, and the distance is not realized half as much as when one encircles a running track for an hour or so. Many men fail to compete in these runs on the

The Hounds.—Taking a Fence.

supposition that they are short-winded, and have not the endurance to withstand the effects of a five-mile chase. This is no criterion, for the successful competition of sprinters and short-distance men has proved that all classes of runners can compete with ease and success. The pleasantest features of this sport are the social intercourse, and the feeling that one is not compelled to endure the hardships of a contest; for the race from the "break" usually narrows down to the six fastest men in the pack.

In the past, college hare and hounds chases have been confined to the fall; but any number of fellows thus inclined can enjoy this sport at any season of the year. Those who are accustomed to the routine work of chest weights and dumb-bells should take part in this out-door exercise, by going out for a five-mile spin twice a week, and, on the return, experience the reaction of a cold shower-bath.

## HINTS FOR YOUNG PEDESTRIANS.

### BY CHARLES M. SKINNER.

IF I could inspire ten wide-awake young fellows with a fondness for pedestrian exercise, I should be quite satisfied to jot down some hints on walking tours, suggested out of an experience of many excursions, aggregating several thousand miles of walking.

A self-reliant lad of good constitution should be able to get along by himself for a week or two, and to find his way through almost any part of the United States without other assistance than civil speech and a small map; and if he is not a self-reliant lad, I know of few things that will do more to develop his pluck, and cultivate a habit of thinking and acting for himself, than walking. Mind, I do not mean walking about a sawdust ring with the object of scoring a higher number of miles than some other contestant; for, while admitting the value of non-professional track-athletics as an educator of nerve and muscle, it is to be remembered that nerves and muscles are kept on a strain that often produces bad effects when the walk is over; then, too, in plodding over dull ground or empty floors the thoughts are tied down to the work and the surroundings, instead of being free to roam, as when the walker is in open air and in the midst of beautiful scenery.

In the first place, you want at least a week for your trip. If you have more time to give, you will be in better trim the longer you walk, as you should aim to increase your distance a little every day. Many people unaccustomed to long walks are exhausted by a ten-mile tramp; but by beginning, say with seven or eight miles, and increasing a mile or so daily, walkers become able to pace off forty miles a day and to be none the worse for it. The object of a pedestrian trip is not, however, to ascertain how much or how fast you can walk, but to see the country, gain new experiences, and enjoy yourself. Of course, in order to do this you must attain a reasonable degree of speed and endurance, otherwise you will find walking a poky affair. To find yourself at night near the place you left in the morning is discouraging, for you will begin to consider life too short to see much without the assistance of horses and railroad trains.

Lay out your route before you start, calculate your expenses, and supply yourself with money enough to meet them, as well as to provide for contingencies. Arrange for the reception of letters at various points, allowing two days between the time of writing and of receiving, for distances over one hundred and under five hundred miles from home. By planning your trip before starting, as you may with the aid of maps and guide-books, you will know exactly what you are undertaking, and will avoid mistakes and confusion. Be sure that you know where you are going, and that you are posted as to the points of interest along the line of march.

Do not encumber yourself with useless luggage. If you carry more than three or four pounds of "traps," you will be tempted to turn about and take them home before you have been more than two hours on your journey. If you intend to camp out every night, you must be content to go heavily weighted, and to put up with many discomforts. You will sleep cold, you will get wet, you will be obliged to carry a tent, hatchet, pan, pot, cup, knife, fork, spoon, and some provisions; and you will be inclined to doubt if the fun equals the trouble, unless you accompany a jolly party, and have the whole summer before you. Here is my whole equipment for tours of any length; it is all I took on a trip across the continent, and were I to visit Europe I should add nothing to it: —

(1) A soft leather satchel, about ten by twelve inches, slung from the shoulder by a strap. It contains (2) a gossamer rubber overcoat, (3) a nightgown, (4) a collar, (5) a neck-tie, (6) a guide-book, or map, (7) postal cards, (8) comb, (9) toothbrush, (10) "telescope" cup; and room is still left for packing small minerals or photographs of places that I visit. In my pockets I carry (11) a watch, (12) sketch-book, (13) pencils, (14) knife, (15) diary, (16) toothpicks, (17) handkerchief, (18) money, (19) and a book for reading during bad weather and at inns in the evening. I also carry (20) a stout cane, which gets to be a companionable sort of thing, and may be of service as a weapon. It is worth carrying for the sense of protection you receive from it, if for no other reason. The rubber overcoat is more than a comfort in

showery weather. The nightgown should be indispensable to everybody; for it is unhealthful and uncleanly to wear the same clothing day and night. Even when compelled to sleep in barns — and there are worse beds than a hay-mow — I laid aside at night every vestige of clothing worn during the day, allowing it to air and dry thoroughly until morning. It is a luxury to slip out of your dusty clothes, damp with perspiration; it is pleasant to find them fresh and serviceable when you awake. Clear water is the best adjunct to a toothbrush in the care of the teeth. Soap and towels you find everywhere, so there is no need for taking them. By all means carry a note-book, or diary, and make a daily jotting of your distances and adventures. Though you write but five or six lines a day, those little hints will serve in after years to strengthen memories of what will probably be classed among the happiest days of your life. So with the sketch-book. The roughest and hastiest of my sketches, though of interest to nobody but myself, calls up a hundred circumstances, and puts me back among the hills in a twinkling. Be earnest in your sketching, and let your drawing, although but an outline, be as true as you can make it. My sketch-book is carried in a large pocket inside my coat.

Now as to clothes. It is plain that you should not set out upon a two-hundred-mile walk dressed in broadcloth, kid gloves, and patent leathers. Take your every-day suit, see that all the pockets are sound, and the buttons sewed on tightly. Be sure that your shoes are thick-soled, well oiled and broken in; and, if you are going to climb mountains, tell the cobbler to put soft iron nails into the heels instead of hard iron or steel, for the latter become smooth and slippery, making your footing unreliable on steep ledges. There is no need of suggesting that you may paddle about barefooted now and then. You will be sure to do that before you have been a day from home; but take smooth roads for it. Bathe your feet every night, and if they are a little tender put soap on your stockings. You will see from my inventory that I carry no stockings except those that I wear. It is more convenient to wear out the pair you start with, washing them now and then, than to carry extra ones. When they are no longer serviceable, throw them away and buy new ones. You may buy them at country stores for fifteen cents. Wear a flannel shirt with gauze underclothing next to the skin. Let the shirt be one of those convenient arrangements with a rolling collar that you can turn down your neck on state occasions, placing over it a linen or paper collar, and a scarf. As the collar and tie conceal all traces of the shirt, nobody knows that you are not arrayed in the finest linen. How do I get my shirt washed? In this way: my nightgown is arranged with collar buttons, and I conceal the front with the collar and scarf, wearing it in place of my shirt while the laundress is scrubbing the dust out of that garment. Flannel shirts need washing but seldom where underclothing is worn, a good shaking often sufficing to get the dust out of them. The nightgown, collar, handkerchief, and underclothing should be washed and ironed for you within eight hours, if you make the laundress understand that you can wait no longer for them.

You will find it so difficult to organize a pedestrian party, that you may as well make up your mind at the outset to go alone. For a day or so you may feel the lack of company; but it will take only a short time to accustom yourself to it, and you will find great delight in the absolute liberty

*Trampers in the Adirondacks.*

you will enjoy. I have never succeeded in finding a companion for a longer excursion than twenty-five miles. No matter what plans are made in advance, at the last moment one pedestrian finds himself up to his ears in business, another has a sore toe, and another has paid his tailor's bill and hasn't a dollar left. I have long given up hope of walking in company; but one is seldom lonely where nature is beautiful, and there is always enough to think about without talking. Even in seemingly well-assorted parties, if one of the number proves to be lazy, or sulky, or dissents from schemes in which the majority concur, or cannot walk fast, or wishes to linger in uninteresting places for selfish reasons, or is always expressing dissatisfaction with the route, or complains loudly at the little privations of travel that should be subjects of merriment instead of melancholy, or has some hobby that he indulges, to loss of interest in his walk, or is vulgar or vicious in his talk or habits, the whole trip may be spoiled. There should be in a party the cheerfulness, delight in nature, and singleness of purpose, that you would feel alone; and it is difficult to find this, for wherever people are assembled together, differences of opinion arise.

Supposing you have started upon your tramp. The sun shines, flowers and foliage sweeten the air, birds sing in the wood yonder, the brook bubbles its cooling music beside the road, the distant hills are clear and blue. Very likely you have seen the landscape hundreds of times before, but it has a new charm now; for you are, perhaps for the first time in your life, absolutely free. Steal into some cornfield by the wayside, and stand on your head for a few minutes to relieve the immense enthusiasm that this feeling is certain to awaken, and resume your walk. You have eaten a hearty breakfast, and your appetite is, no doubt, healthy enough to fill your landlords with some anxiety when you begin your depredations in their dining-rooms; but do not eat a big dinner at noon. If your means are limited, you cannot afford it; if your time is limited, the hour you will spend at the table will be a heavy sacrifice; and if your stomach is heavily loaded, you cannot walk as blithely as you did before dinner. Take your heartiest meal later in the day. At noon, or thereabout, knock at some farmhouse door; and ask for bread and milk. You will receive enough for three, your bill may reach fifteen cents, but it is more likely to be ten, and you will be in better trim to continue the walk than if you had been eating meat, vegetables, and pie. I have often obtained lunches at farmhouses that were almost equal in variety and abundance to a regular dinner. Here is what a man in the Catskills once set before me, after apologizing for the emptiness of his pantry: cold meat, preserved fruit, cake, bread, pot-cheese, and fresh cider. Now guess the amount of his bill. Thirteen cents! Don't be bashful about asking for a bowl of bread and milk, at least in any farmhouse of respectable size and appearance. It is the one thing sure to be found: it is nourishing; and though the charge for it, if one is made, is so low that you feel compunctions of conscience for not paying it twice, remember that money goes farther than in town, while the lunch costs your worthy host the merest trifle. For dessert, help yourself to fruit and berries from the wayside. If benighted, storm-bound, or astray, you will have little difficulty in getting the good farmer folk to give you a lodging over night, offering to pay them, of course, for their trouble. They will perplex you with their curiosity; but if you talk cheerfully and frankly, they will like you, and your stay will be pleasant.

Unless you are well supplied with money, do not stop over night in cities and large towns upon your route. Arrange your trip so that you can pass through them, and put up at the tavern in a village beyond. Not in the suburbs, for there the hotels are wretched, but in some country settlement; there the beds will be clean, the tables well-supplied, the charges will be moderate, and you will not be compelled to "dress up" to an alarming extent on account of the company you will meet. Always ascertain the amount of your bill in advance. If you are compelled to stop in a city, it will be wiser, unless your stay is of several days, to engage rooms and pay for only such meals as you have, than to lodge in a pretentious hotel where you pay full day's board if you are there only two hours. Should you lose your way, or find yourself belated and compelled to spend the night in the open air, contrive some sort of covering that shall keep off the dew. A tree is better than nothing. Do not light a fire unless the night is cold, for it will attract bugs, moths, and flies by hundreds; but if you do light one, sleep with your feet towards it, and make sure that nothing in the vicinity is likely to catch the flame. I doubt if your first night on the ground be passed in very sound sleep. You will better enjoy thinking and telling about your experience afterward, than undergoing it at the time. Mysterious murmurs will be heard in the branches; soft footfalls and gliding noises will come from thickets; night birds, crickets, katydids, and frogs will talk persistently; now and then you will start up prepared to affirm that you heard a whisper; you will wonder if there are snakes, skunks, weasels, and rats in the vicinity; and it may be some hours before you realize that the queer noises are only produced by wind and harmless insects; then your tired head will sink upon the grass, you will thrash about and partly wake at intervals, and will presently sit up to rub your stiff elbows and discover that it is morning. Before lying down, remove all hard things except watch and money from your pockets, as they will press into your flesh when you lie upon them, and hurt you. Then turn up your coat collar and button your clothing well about you, for dew will fall and the night be chilly. If your hat or cap is too good to sleep in, tie your handkerchief about your head. Ease your feet by partly unlacing or unbuttoning your shoes, and be sure that your shirt is not tight about the neck. Use your satchel or nightgown as a pillow, your rubber overcoat as a blanket, a heap of grass or leaves as a mattress. You will rest more comfortably if you will make a hollow in the ground about three inches deep, for your shoulder to slip into, and another like it for the hip. I don't recommend sleeping out of doors "for fun." I have tried board floors, wagons, and freight cars, and have found them, with a little dressing of weeds and grass, pleasanter beds than bare ground.

As to a "stamping-ground," all parts of the country offer attractive pedestrian routes, though I should fancy that the plains and prairies might become monotonous to the walker. Among regions favorable for walking, I can, from experience, recommend the White and Green Mountains, Catskills, the Lehigh region, Hudson, Connecticut, Housatonic, Delaware, Potomac, and Shenandoah valleys, the New England coast from Cape Cod to Portland, Western New York and Niagara, and the regions about Montreal and Quebec. These districts are penetrated by railroads and the telegraph, so that in case of accident, sickness, or loss of funds, you could return or communicate with home at once.

The walker may pleasantly vary his route by returning over different roads from those upon which he set forth. Here is a sample route, taken from one of my summer tramps: Boston to Alton Bay, N. H., across Lake Winnepesaukee by steamer, Centre Harbor, Campton, Pemigewasset valley, the Pool, Basin, Flume, Franconia Notch, Profile, Echo Lake, Franconia, Bethlehem, Fabyan's, Mt. Deception, Mt. Washington, Crawford bridle path over the Presidential range to the Crawford House, White Mountain Notch, Bartlett, Glen Road and return, Iron Mountain, North Conway, Lake Ossipee, Portland, Salem, Lynn, and Boston. It is sometimes practicable to establish one's headquarters in the centre of an interesting region, striking out in various directions from that point. Thus, in the Catskills, the village of Hunter affords a convenient point of departure for Hunter Mountain, Stony Clove, Kaaterskill Clove, Plattekill Clove, South and North Mountains, Cairo, Windham, Lexington, and Grand Gorge.

The young traveller who has the entire summer before him, and a purse long enough to attempt such an undertaking safely, may adapt the following route to his liking by cutting from or adding to the list of interesting points, going over some portions of the country by rail, and perhaps accepting the numerous invitations to ride that farmers, travelling from town to town, extend to people they overtake upon the road. Starting up the Hudson River from New York visit Sunnyside, the home of Irving; Tarrytown and its quaint Dutch church; Sing Sing and the State prison there; the military school and old forts at West Point; Storm King, highest of the Hudson hills; Newburg and Washington's headquarters; Saugerties, from which point a detour can be made, embracing some of the finest portions of the Catskills, returning to the Hudson River at Catskill village; Albany and the Capitol; Troy; Saratoga and its famous springs; Glen's Falls; Fort William Henry; down Lake George by steamer; Ticonderoga and its historic ruins; down Lake Champlain by steamer, stopping at Port Henry or Essex for a brief run into the Adirondack region; Port Kent and Au Sable Chasm; Burlington; up the Winooski, ascending Camel's Hump and stopping at Montpelier; Wells River; Woodstock, N. H., from which point make a tour of the White Mountains, similar to that just outlined; Boston, or Connecticut valley, to New York.

There! Some of the grandest and most beautiful scenery in the world is yours to enjoy upon this trip. Or, if that programme is not sufficiently ambitious, you may omit the walk across Vermont, and extend your trip from Port Kent to Montreal and Quebec, descending into the White Mountain region of the North.

The interest of your walk will be much increased if you will glance through the history of the region you intend to explore; or, if you have a scientific turn, you might post yourself on the geology, mineralogy, or botany of the country.

# OUT-OF-DOOR GYMNASTICS.

### BY JOHN GRAHAM,
*Athletic Manager Boston Athletic Association and Ex-Superintendent Charlesbank Gymnasium.*

TO the healthy boy or girl, exercise is always attractive. It is also helpful and strengthening. The practice of gymnastics develops the muscles, tones the system, and yields toughened sinews in place of debilitating fat. The gymnasium is the means to this end; its simple or complicated appliances alike affording that opportunity for systematic development that modern gymnastics aims to secure.

But fresh air is the chief tonic. An out-of-door gymnasium, where such is possible, is then an even better means toward the acquiring of muscle and sinew, strength and health, than one in-doors.

Realizing this fact, the "powers that be" in the city of Boston instituted in the strip of park known as the Charlesbank, an open-air gymnasium, fitting it up with the appliances that give the best exercise — chest weights, pulleys, parallel bars, horizontal bars, climbing poles, vaulting poles, giant strides, jumping boxes, jumping standards and ropes, sand bags, quoits, dumb-bells, hurdles, swings, perpendicular and inclined ladders, rope and Jacob's ladders, flying rings, inclined and perpendicular poles, trapezes, breast bars, balance swings, etc.

This out-of-door "gym" is almost in the heart of the city. It occupies a space in the fine embankment along the Charles River near to the bridge that Longfellow made famous. It is free to the public; and a systematic attempt for practical instruction has been attempted with excellent results.

A class of boys was formed for the purpose of experimenting in these class drills under no roof but the sky. Having a large space that was not being occupied for anything in particular, a platform was built upon the ground, made from the plank walks used on the park during the winter. This platform was marked off in spaces, and was found to accommodate about forty in a class. None of the boys was over eighteen years of age; the youngest was fifteen years. All wore a costume consisting of a white shirt, amateur running pants, and rubber-soled shoes.

Every one of these boys worked all day at some light trade; so, to make it convenient, the class was called together at half-past six every alternate evening.

Drills lasted fifteen minutes, each drill being followed by class work in light athletic exercises. The drills were changed every night, so that the boys did not receive the same platform drill once in two weeks. Drills consisted of free movements, Indian clubs, dumb-bells, bar bells, sometimes followed by parallel bars, flying rings, and athletics in the primary exercises. As an experiment I feel sure it was a success. At the beginning it was impossible to have the boys go through these exercises without feeling conscious of the crowd of lookers-on outside, who amused themselves by making personal remarks on the different attitudes of the members of the class. This did not add to the *esprit* of the class, and at last the outside critics were requested to cease their remarks. They readily complied, and after a few days really took as much interest in the exercises as did the scholars themselves. Now, it must be understood that these boys had never attended a gymnasium, so that it was much harder for them to face a large crowd than it would be for boys who had been accustomed to doing their "gym" work in public.

After the novelty had worn off, it was found that the exercises could be made as attractive as are in-door gymnastics, and much more beneficial because of the purer air and the pleasant surroundings.

It is in the open air that one attains the very foundation for physical strength; and if this out-of-door exercise is but carried on systematically, it will prove of the utmost importance to growing bodies.

*The Medicine Ball. (On Top of Head.)*

The field for out-door gymnastics is wide; people are beginning to see the value of parks and breathing places; and gymnasiums in these parks are of the greatest value, both physically and morally. The exercises that are carried on in-doors can be repeated out-doors when the same apparatus is at hand.

The German Government, through its school board, makes gymnastic work almost compulsory, and has it carried on out-of-doors. There are a number of out-of-door gymnasiums, and these are attended by all the school children. Each gymnasium is provided with a director-general of gymnastics. The gymnasiums are built about the same as the Charlesbank Gymnasium.

The Medicine Ball. (On One Arm.)

At the Charlesbank the giant stride is a popular piece of apparatus. This consists of a stout pole fixed in the ground, with a revolving plate on its head; hung from the plate are ropes, with handles attached to them; there are four, six, or eight ropes, and these are grasped separately, while each performer pushes on the ground with his feet until all attain sufficient momentum to swing around without touching the ground. For the children, instead of ropes, ribbons are used. As the children march around the pole the ribbons are plaited around it, making a very pretty sight when the ribbons are of different colors. By reversing the order of marching, the ribbons unwind from the pole. The heavier apparatus is very valuable as a strengthener of the grasp, and assists in the development of the chest and abdominal muscles.

All the special apparatus can be used out-doors. Of this, special mention may be made of the Neck Developer. It is a plain band of canvas with a cross piece over the ears, the whole being brought to a point in front of the forehead. Fastened to the canvas is a slip-hook, which can be attached to the handle of a chest weight. By standing and facing sideways (left and right), and back to the weight, the muscles of the neck can be exercised.

Another piece of apparatus is the Medicine Ball, the invention of Mr. Roberts, of the Boston Y. M. C. A. Gymnasium. This is a large, leather-covered ball weighing about ten pounds. The mode of exercising is to pass it from one to the other from different positions, with both hands, each hand separate — from over the head, between the legs, from the right and left side, and numerous other ways. When used as it should be, it is one of the best exercises known, both as a strengthener of the whole muscular system and a means of recreation.

Another popular exercise is the Spring Board. This apparatus is customarily used in connection with the Jumping Rope, or Buck. In the former the gymnasts run to the Spring Board, and leap over the rope at different heights. When this is done in connection with the Buck, in much the same manner as leap-frog, finishing with a roll over on the mat, the exercise it affords the legs is most admirable.

Another piece of apparatus not found in the in-door gymnasium is the Tilting Ladder. This appliance is a source of great enjoyment to those who use it, and is a very popular piece of apparatus. It is arranged so that it can be used as well by the small boys as by the men, for the pin through the centre can be drawn out and placed lower down on the posts supporting it. The sensation of flying through the air induces many to try it, for it is a fact that an apparatus that has any swing in connection with it is the most popular. The Tilting Ladder acts in a like manner with the Giant Stride, as far as developing the muscles is concerned.

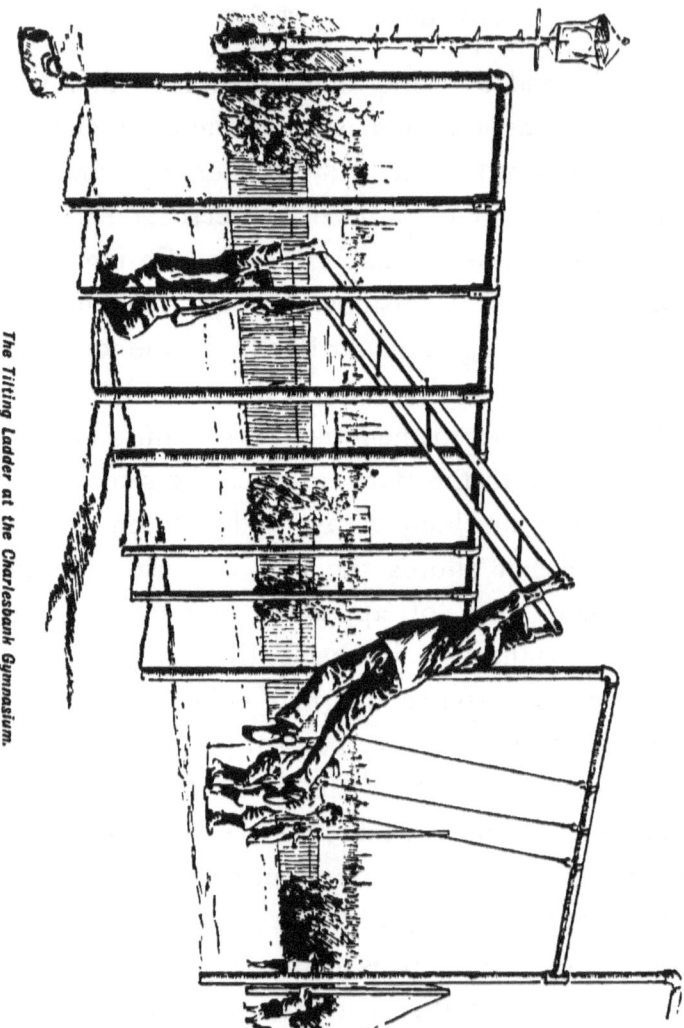

*The Tilting Ladder at the Charlesbank Gymnasium.*

The Jacob's Ladder, or, as the boys have termed it, the "Razzle Dazzle," is another piece of apparatus not frequently seen in a gymnasium. This ladder is hung from the framework by a swivel hook, and is not fastened in the ground, but is allowed to swing loose. The rungs of the ladder are about eighteen inches apart, and fastened together by a chain or steel bar, through the centre of the rung. This arrangement allows the rungs to swing loose. The mode of exercising with this apparatus is to grasp a rung at the full reach, and lift the body from the ground to a rung opposite the waist line; then the legs are spread apart, and come to a sitting position on the rung. The hands grasp another rung, higher up the ladder, the legs are spread apart, and so one pulls himself to the

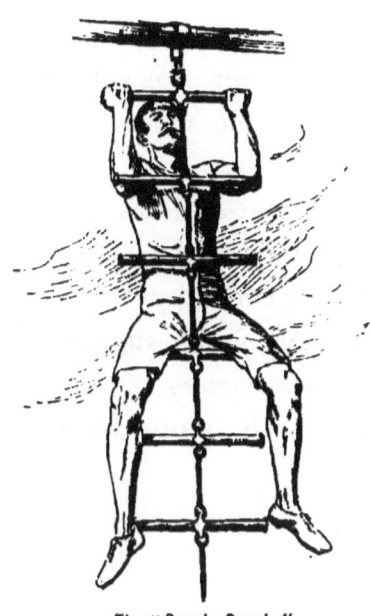

The "Razzle Dazzle."

top of the ladder. This is splendid exercise for the muscles of the hips and thighs, while the back and arms also come in for a great deal of exercise.

The interest in out-door work is growing every year, as the attendance at the Charlesbank shows. When the gymnasium was first opened, it was looked upon as a place for fun; now it is esteemed as a place where the needs of the muscular system are attended to systematically.

The success of this Boston out-of-door gymnasium should lead to the adoption of the system in other cities; while the fact that such appliances for open-air exercise are possible should suggest to inventive and wide-awake boys a means of furnishing fun and exercise, with a wide scope for their ingenuity and skill.

# HOW TO MAKE AN OUT-DOOR GYMNASIUM.

### BY WILLIAM F. GARCELON.

GIVE a Yankee boy a suggestion, and his native ingenuity will devise a way to surmount any difficulties that may arise during his attempt to follow and develop it. Every boy delights in exercise; but the solid ground and his own body do not offer chance for enough diversity of action to satisfy his restlessness, and consequently we find him climbing fences and "shinning" trees at every opportunity. There is something fascinating about a gymnasium to the young lad and older youth, but unfortunately gymnastic facilities are not available to a great part of energetic Young America. Few boys, however, in the country realize how easily home-made apparatus can be constructed. A few suggestions as to the building and equipment of a rough-and-ready out-of-door gymnasium such as any boy can make for himself, may be adapted by the reader to the circumstances and facilities at hand.

Every boy knows what is required for the construction of the ordinary swing. If trees are near by, they may be made very useful, as they are often so formed that they will furnish support for a beam or joist to which the ropes may be attached.

Often a single large branch will support the pendent apparatus.

Or, if in-doors, there is always some convenient beam in barn or shed which can be utilized.

If made rightly, the swing may serve both as a swing and as a trapeze. The trapeze bar should be from an inch to an inch and a half in diameter. The handle of a broken pitchfork, hoe, or rake is often used.

Notch the bar near the ends to prevent the rope from slipping; hang the bar so that it can just be reached from the ground, and the trapeze is ready for use. Ropes reaching almost to the ground may be fastened to the bar, and there you have a complete swing and trapeze combined. When the trapeze is used, the lower swing may be laid aside.

A still better arrangement is to have the trapeze bar a foot or six inches above reach. Attach iron rings to ropes, and hang them from the trapeze bar so that they will be about as high as the head. Numberless little combination tricks can be performed with this double apparatus. Rings can be purchased at one dollar a pair.

If, however, the rings are not readily procured a handy boy can make them himself of plaited rope; while not having the stiffness of the iron rings, these will serve the purpose.

Of course, the rings may be detached from the trapeze at any time. Thus we may have with little or no expense, trapeze, swinging rings, and an ordinary swing.

These equipments require, of course, some overhanging support.

What boy has not circled the cross-bar of some old barn door? Yet, this is simply the horizontal bar; and the horizontal bar is one of the most popular pieces of apparatus in a gymnasium. The best bars are made of hickory, and are one and a half or two inches in diameter. The ends are square and when regular uprights are used, there are small holes at the ends for the insertion of the supporting pins.

A very good bar can be purchased of dealers

*A Wrestling Match.*

in gymnastic goods for two dollars. But boys may make a bar for themselves out of maple or hickory, or by using a large pitchfork or hoe-handle. Home-made bars should, however, always be tested thoroughly before being used, and should not be used by very large or heavy boys.

The greatest difficulty arises in fixing the bar firmly. If an old tree is at hand, a hole about an inch and a half deep may be cut out, into which one end of the bar should exactly fit.

Then, if a large post or an ordinary piece of joist can be firmly planted at a distance of four or five feet from the tree, the other end of the bar may be inserted in that. The planted post should be well propped to prevent spreading. The bar should be about five feet from the ground.

All the feats on the horizontal bar, except a few of the more difficult and dangerous, may be performed with the bar at that height. But a tree is not always available, and the boy must often depend for one support upon the side of a house or barn or upon a fence. If he squares the end of his bar, he can easily arrange a support by nailing firmly to the house a piece of thick board or plank, with an opening cut to receive the end of the bar.

The board should be thick enough to prevent the bar from coming out of the opening when it bends with the weight of the performer. The other end, of course, may be supported by upright joist or plank as described above.

If a rough mattress of hay or straw cannot be made, it would be well to loosen the earth on one side of the bar to save any unnecessary jars; for beginners are quite liable to fall upon shoulders or back.

Jumping standards are most easily made. Place two upright sticks firmly in the ground. Drive in nails, an inch apart, allowing them to project an inch or two for holding the cross-bar. The uprights should be six feet apart, and the ground in front should be firm and solid in order to assure a good take-off for the jump. A small stick is generally used as a cross-bar; although many use a small rope, to the ends of which weights are attached to keep it taut.

A handkerchief or white paper placed on the cross-bar aids the jumper. These standards may also be used for hurdling, pole-vaulting, or high diving. For the diving, a thick, soft mat is necessary.

The vaulting-horse is a piece of apparatus not

well known to those who have not attended the gymnasium. But a great variety of exercises may be done upon it, and a rough one may be easily constructed, especially in the country. Secure a smooth log about five feet long and from twelve to twenty inches in diameter, and after rounding it at the ends, insert four substantial and firm legs, about two and a half or three feet long. One set should be about a foot from one end of the log, and the other two legs about two feet from the other end.

This log may be covered with canvas, under which a little straw or hay may be placed, or it can be used without a covering. By attaching curved pieces of wood to the log, pommels are supplied which will greatly add to the usefulness of the apparatus and to the number of feats that may be performed upon it.

All kinds of vaulting and many easy tricks are done on the horse.

None of this apparatus can be constructed without perseverance and patience; for trifling difficulties will nearly always arise, which, owing to the different conditions under which boys may work, cannot be considered here.

# HINTS FOR YACHTSMEN.

### BY CAPTAIN JULIUS A. PALMER, JR.,
*Of the American Shipmasters' Association.*

### I. — ON BOARD.

GLORIOUS sport is yachting! It is, however, a pastime of recent introduction; many of those who are not considered old remember when its nucleus was no more than occasional "sailboats," owned by private parties, or let for excursions; now, from the mosquito fleet of some sheltered bay to the five-hundred-ton steam yacht, able to circumnavigate the globe, the shores of both sides of the Atlantic swarm with craft of every size and description, manned and managed by volunteer sailors.

# HINTS FOR YACHTSMEN.

The earth's surface is, to the extent of two-thirds, covered with water, and there has always been a proportion of the human race living upon the ocean. Yachting is, therefore, a perfectly natural development; and its possibilities are, in the future, greater rather than less. This being the case, just as the boy who enters a store looks at the European buyer, the head salesman, or the manager of some department, as the holders of positions to which he may aspire, so from his catboat along shore he may see the seagoing yacht, under steam or sail, taking her departure for the broad ocean, and form for himself the resolution that by the time he can hope to have such a one,

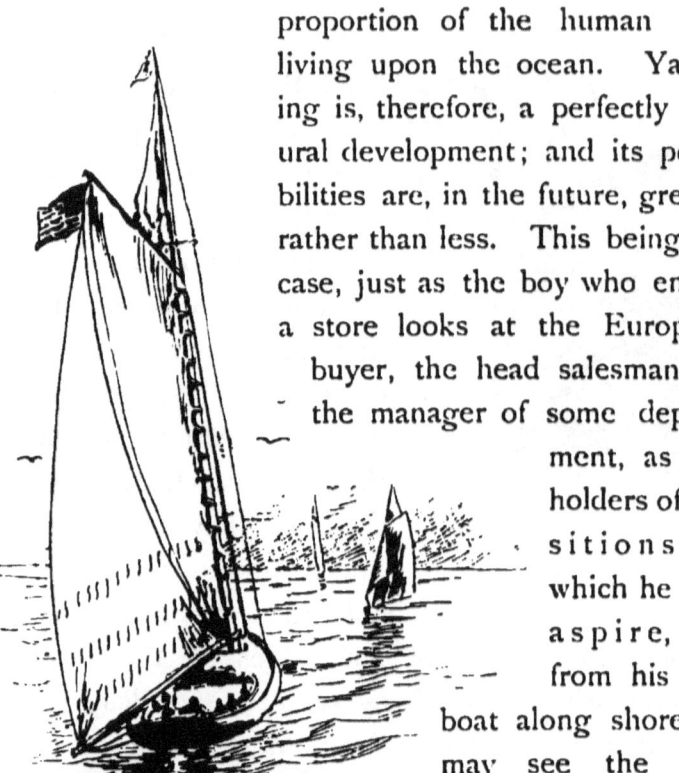

*Off for a Cruise.*

he will know all that is essential to her proper management.

The Concord philosopher, Emerson, tells us to fit ourselves for any position, and God will send the opportunity; ignorance is no disgrace, but it is a shame to be willing to remain ignorant; so the young man who owns a twenty-foot boat may

master, and even practise, principles which will make him a better yachtsman, and, if he persevere, a thorough sailor.

Take first the mariner's compass, for it is the most essential of any of his belongings; we can cross the ocean without a chart, but not without a compass.

> "When ministers try poor sailors to teach,
> Compass, no chart, is the figure of speech."

*Off Sandy Hook.*

I was once on a yacht in Salem Harbor; the skipper was a man of experience; it had been foggy, then had cleared a trifle, with a light breeze; and as night was coming on, all sail was made for home — that is, according to the bearings relied on by the skipper. I was not just satisfied, and took the liberty, although only a guest, to ask him if he had a compass.

"Oh, yes!" he said; "there's a box-compass down in my bunk."

I hastened below, and on my return startled him with the information that he was then steering due east. The schooner was put about at once.

Now, the nautical custom is, in fair weather or foul, along shore or on the deep sea, to never lose sight of the lubber's-point of your compass; the proper place for a steering-compass is just forward of the wheel or tiller; if your yacht is roomy aft, a metallic binnacle can be fixed at the right spot; but if you have only a cat-boat, a neat box holding a small compass can be secured to the slide over the companion way, or entrance to the cuddy; thus, when you are sailing, you will naturally keep your eye on the fine black mark in line with the keel, and not fail to know the course you are steering. The mariner's compass has the needle fixed to the back of the card, so that this latter moves on its centre; the compass in use by engineers and surveyors has a fixed card, over which the needle rotates.

Then, as the Government examiners in Great Britain say, "You must be well up on the compass." "Oh! but I could always box the compass," interrupts one of my readers. To begin at one point, and name them all until you reach the same again, is pretty practice for the memory, and that is about all. You should know your compass just as you know your watch; the face of the latter is divided into hours, minutes, and often seconds; that of the former, besides the points, into degrees, minutes, and seconds. Of late, it is customary to use the latter, rather than the points, so that a vessel's course might be given as N. 45° E., instead of N. E., the one term being equal to the other. Space does not permit further illustration; but for a few cents a compass card, marked for both degrees and points, may be bought, and a little study will enable you to master this, the very a b c of nautical knowledge.

By the compass and chart, the distance of your yacht from any vessel, or any point of land, may

*The Winner of the Race.*

be found; this may seem paradoxical, yet it is so simple that it can be explained in a few words. Suppose that Nahant, east point, bears due west, and at the same moment the south point of Marblehead is seen bearing due north; now, is it not perfectly clear that if you rule a line on the chart, running in the directions given from each of these points of land, at the very spot where those two lines cross, your yacht must be lying? Or again, suppose you are running past Boston Light, visible twenty miles, bound for the north shore of the bay, how far are you from it? The first bearing of it you have is W. N. W., and you rule a line from the Light running indefinitely from that direction out to sea; in about an hour it has changed its bearing, as you have sailed north, say five miles, so that it now bears W. S. W.; rule another line to correspond; now go to the edge of the chart, and extend your dividers five miles, and move each arm of the instruments along the two lines you have ruled; there will be but one place where the distance between the two ruled lines is equal to just five miles; at its northern limit is the spot where your yacht is; at its southern is the place where she was when you took the bearing.

The compass-card has no needle affixed to its under side, but it is useful to you in this way: run a stout thread through the centre, and put a knot in one end, letting the other remain to a length of about fifteen inches; now, when you wish to know in what direction any place is from another, go to the chart, put the card plumb with the chart's projection; that is, let the north point on the card be at the exact north, etc., and keeping it thus, by moving either the east and west points on a parallel of latitude, or the north and south points on a meridian of longitude, when the string runs in a straight line between the two places, on the margin of the compass-card is the true course.

When sailing your boat as close to the wind as she will lie, if the sea is rough, look over the stern and you will notice that the wake, instead of being right aft, is to windward; slanting, as a landsman would say. This means that she is making leeway, or that the wind is pressing her away from the course to which her head points, so that although the bow is headed in a certain direction, the whole body of the boat is sagging off to leeward; if you glance at the compass as you look at the wake, you will obtain the amount of this deflection from your steered course, and allow it always away from the wind.

Every ambitious yachtsman should begin at once to learn both seamanship and navigation; there are excellent manuals, in both branches, to be bought at the nautical bookstores. It is better to know too much than too little of your craft; you thus avoid the error of the novice in the use of the compass, who nailed it down at the course he was told to make, simply saying it was the only way — "the thing bobbed round so." You are also spared the danger which attended the amateur master of a new steam yacht, which was found by the inspectors with the safety-valve strapped down; the excuse offered was, that "the hole made such a noise you couldn't talk."

Even in the management of boats, there is much to be learned. Never keep the sheet of a small boat fast when sailing on a wind, if your craft is small; always have a hand stationed at the cleat to which it is belayed, providing your boat is too large to allow you to hold a single turn with your hand. This is the very first principle of sailing a yacht with safety. For, if the breeze freshens, or a squall strikes you, and you slack the sheet of a fore-and-aft sail, it becomes no more than an immense flag, blowing loosely to leeward; your boat cannot capsize, and the sail can be thus lowered or managed.

Directions for fair-weather sailing are perhaps superfluous; but suppose you are caught at quite a distance from land in bad weather; then you may have an opportunity to show your seamanship, for seamen are made only by rough weather and the perils of their calling. Naturally, as a yachtsman, you would run for a harbor, and would choose such a one as would make of the gale a fair wind. But, at a time like this, accidents are likely to befall you; you may lose a rudder; you may be in a "single-sticker," and your only mast may be carried away, or the seas that follow may threaten to swamp you. Now, what can you do? The first and best thing in such cases — that is, a rule which will apply to most of them — is to bring your boat's bow, instead of the stern, to the wind; for by its sharpness she will ride far easier, or divide the combers with less danger to herself. If she is still manageable by the helm, this should be at once done; if not, a small piece of canvas, even an open umbrella, well aft, where some boats carry a little sail called a jigger, will swing her head to the sea. To keep her there,

"An open umbrella will swing her head to the sea."

bend a bucket or tin pail, or more than one of these common utensils, to a line, and throw it over at the bow; the more line you can pay out, the better your sea-anchor will hold, and the resistance of this drag to the water will enable you to ride the seas with perfect ease, all the time drifting, instead of running, toward the haven you have chosen. If the mast — sail and rigging attached — goes by the board, — that is, breaks off and hangs over the side, — cut it loose from your boat, but do not let it go adrift; make one end of a line fast as near the centre of gravity of the wreckage as you can reach, pay out on the line all you can, and make the other end fast at the bow of the boat; now, as you drift, the surface-drag, being to windward of your boat, will meet each sea before it approaches you, and thus you will ride safely in smooth water until you gain a place of refuge, or receive the aid of some of your companions.

By the hints here given, I desire to inspire yachtsmen with ambition for their higher duties. By constantly learning something of one's vocation, its pleasure is enhanced and its utility increased.

## II. — SEA-TERMS.

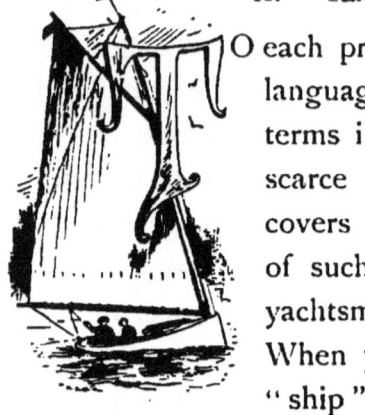

TO each profession belongs its own language. A full list of the terms in use aboard ship could scarce be printed between the covers of this book; but a few of such as would be used by a yachtsman may be mentioned. When you go a-sailing, you first "ship" (put in place) your rudder, and "step" (put in place) your mast; be sure to get both "pintles" directly over their "gudgeons" before you cast off the "painter" or get "under way." Suppose you wish to "weather" some dangerous rock "under your lee," you will haul aft the "sheet," which last term does not refer to a sail, but to the rope which is fast to the "clew" or lower "after" corner of a "fore-and-aft" sail. After you have made a short "board," let us say, on the "starboard tack" — that is, run a short distance with the wind on the right-hand side of your yacht — you will have to "go about," and perhaps can make a "long board" on the "port tack." You are now clear of the land, and can "gybe the boom," so as to let her " go free ; " after " running " out to sea, you put your " helm down " and " luff up," so as to speak one of your companions. If the latter should be a steam yacht, it is the master's duty to " keep out of your way " — that is, so manage his vessel that there shall be no danger to your boat ; a very reasonable rule, since with steam he can go in any direction, while you are dependent upon the wind. But if both yachts are under sail, then the one on the " starboard tack" has the " right of way," and the one on the " port tack " must " give way." I will not even guess at the size or the rig of your yacht, but it is safe to presume that the " clew of the mainsail " is hauled out to the end of a boom ; this would be true of a schooner, a sloop, a British cutter, or a cat-boat. A very few sail-boats now carry " sprit-s'ls " — that is, sails extended to the wind by a light spar, one end of which spreads the head of the sail, while the other is supported by an " eye-splice " in a short length of rope fixed on the mast a few feet from the " gunwale " of the boat. The edge or part of the sail to which the " bolt-rope " is sewed is called the " leech ;" " the head, the foot, the after-leech, and the luff," are the four sides or edges, and any rope

*Rounding the Buoy.*

which hoists anything aloft is called its "halliards." The spar at the head of your mains'l is the "gaff;" and it is sometimes furnished with both "throat halliards," near the mast, and "peak halliards," near to the "after-leech." Your jib, or three-cornered sail forward of the mast, has its "jib halliards;" it also has a "down-haul," while any sail which is set on a boom has an "outhaul." A sail is "furled" when it is taken in and stowed in its place; it is "reefed" when it is reduced in size by gathering in some part of it to the yard or the bolt-rope, tying it there by small ropes fixed in line in the sail itself. These are called "reef-points," while the larger rope which is securely passed in a lashing at the "bolt-rope" is called the "earing." This takes the strain off the "body" (the central cloths of the sail), and is itself restrained from tearing the canvas by being passed through an iron ring worked into the sail. This iron ring is found wherever it is needful for the sail to bear the strain of a rope, and is called a "thimble;" but a piece of rope usually passes around it in a loop, and this entire loop, protected on its inner side by the "thimble," is the "reef cringle." You "carry away" a mast or other spar when it breaks away from its fastening, or when a part of it breaks off. If it simply weakens or becomes unsteady, it is only "sprung."

Let us suppose that in your cruise you are far enough from land to sight a "square-rigged" vessel inward bound; she has "hove to" for a pilot, while near to her may be seen the pilot-boat, usually a small schooner "lying to." The first-named has simply "braced her main yards aback," so that there is as much sail-power forcing her astern as ahead; while the pilot-boat, being desirous to remain for hours where she now lies, has "shortened sail" — that is, reduced it to just enough to keep her hull balanced on the waves, over which she rides with her bow pointing almost into the wind, and drifting off to "leeward."

But the pilot goes to the "bark" (a three-masted vessel with one mast, the "mizzen," rigged just like your sloop, the two others having "yards," crossing the masts, on which are square sails) in a small boat; he seizes hold of the "man-ropes," one on each side of the "Jacob's ladder" hanging over the "lee" side in the "waist," or about half-way from the bow to the stern of the vessel. These ropes are sharply pointed at one end, and at the other they have a knot made not like the one a landsman would make, but squarely built in the very centre of the strands by passing each one of them around the " standing part." and through the " bights " or loops made with the strands.

There are few mechanics on shore that work as incessantly as merchant seamen when at sea. If not engaged in making or taking in sail, they are at work on the ship's hull, its sails or its ropes; and they do in their way as skilful, even as ornamental, work as that executed in silk or worsted by their sisters and sweethearts at home. Watch a sailor handle a rope, and you will notice that he does just the right thing for each emergency; for example, he will hoist the ensign aloft in a small roll, then with a twitch of the halliards he shakes it out, and it floats in the breeze; he will put a running bowline in the end of a rope which is "rove" through a "block" at the "mast-head," and lower himself safely to the deck, when a landsman could not even trust himself to knot the rope securely. For each purpose he has its appropriate "hitch, bend, splice, seizing, or lashing." Far more of this ornamental and seaman-like work might be done aboard yachts, so that, however small the craft, she might show that she was owned by a sailor. I thought in beginning this article that I might possibly give some directions as to this work, but it is not easily explained without engravings. Mr. R. H. Dana, a Boston boy who went two years before the mast, and wrote a famous book about it, also published a work entitled *The Seaman's Friend*, in which may be found plates of great use to those who wish to learn how to handle ropes. It is also the most correct and comprehensive manual of seamanship as practised on sea-going vessels that has ever been printed. We should all be proud of the fact that it was the work of a man of education, for many years a celebrated lawyer, who followed the seaman's vocation for the benefit of his health, but perfected himself in every duty of his station. So great is the fascination of the life of a sailor, that Mr. Dana himself said to me, within two years of his death, that he could not go to one of our wharves and see a square-rigged vessel without feeling all the old longing to go to sea.

## III. — STARBOARD AND PORT.

WHEN you go a-sailing, remember that every vessel has a forward and an after part; the former is the bow, the latter the stern: these names are constantly applied aboard ship; thus, a rope is made fast forward of the mainmast, or a boat is ordered astern. Every vessel has also a right and a left side: the former is starboard, the latter port, or larboard; and in familiar speech the two sets of men, or watches, have been sometimes called Starbowlines and Larbowlines. The words right and left are not sea-terms: if a man were to say that his bunk was on the larboard side (although port is more usual) he would be set down as a mariner of experience; but if he said it was to the left, he would be considered a landsman.

No one unacquainted with nautical life can realize how incessantly these two words are used at sea; for the jibboom, there must be starboard and port guys; the ship must have a starboard and port anchor, a starboard and port light; square-rigged vessels, or those with yards, have most of their rigging alike on both sides, so we prefix to orders the word starboard or port, unless we use instead the terms weather and lee. It has been proposed to substitute the ordinary words right and left; but while with steamers or yachts no inconvenience would result, aboard sea-going vessels such a change involves far more than can be apparent to any landsman. An order to overhaul the right clewline might be ambiguous, but "Overhaul the starboard clewline" is plain. "Is the wheel a-port?" cannot be misunderstood; but how about "Is the wheel a-left?"

"Right your wheel" means to bring the rudder in line with the keel. All ancient steering-gear was identical with that used by small boats to-day, or an arm of wood fast to the rudder-head; every boy knows that to carry this tiller to the starboard side brings the rudder to the opposite side, and thus the bow of the boat is turned to port; the first improvements in steering conformed to this rule, and the wheel itself moved to the right or to the left, so that in old vessels a channel may be seen worn into the deck, where the man at the wheel has followed the tiller. Stationary wheels came, moving the rudder in the direction indicated by the wheel; but the terms were not changed. So that to this day the man moves his wheel exactly to the contrary of the order, following the old rule that the vessel must go to the side opposite that to which the helm is put.

The terms port and starboard only are in use on the sea: two vessels approaching must port the helm; if sailing-vessels, the one on the starboard tack has right of way; if steamers, one whistle indicates that each keeps to starboard; two to port; at night a green light is carried on the starboard side, a red one to port; the distinction being easily recalled if you remember that port wine is red.

# THE ART OF SWIMMING.

### BY HARRY E. ROSE.

SWIMMING is an art so manly, so graceful, and so useful, that no one ever regrets the trouble of learning. And every one can learn, unless he be physically infirm or naturally a coward.

Dr. Franklin truthfully said: "The only obstacle to the acquirement and improvement in this necessary and life-preserving art is fear." The coward had better stay out of the water. He is safer on land. But he is not necessarily a coward who is afraid to plunge boldly into unknown water — such a reluctance is natural; the best swimmer, unless he be foolhardy, would not do that. Some of the best swimmers have learned in shallow creeks, have practised alone until skilled, and then polished their self-education in deep water.

The first lesson should be taken in a tideless river or quiet stream, the depth of which you have previously studied. On entering the water, wet your head and neck thoroughly; and before submerging the body stand for a few minutes knee-deep.

Having fixed your eye on a favorable spot, advance into the stream until breast-high. Now face the shore, and prepare for striking out. Lie gently on your breast, keeping head and neck upright, breast distended, and back bent inward. Withdraw the legs from the bottom, and immediately strike them out, not downward, but horizontally; strike forward with the arms simultaneously with the feet, holding the hands like the blade of an oar when in action, fingers closed, the thumb placed by the side of the first finger, a little below the surface; draw them back again while gathering up the legs for a second attempt; and thus push forward, making use of the hands and feet alternately. The farther forward you reach, the faster you will swim. The secret of a good stroke is to kick out with the legs wide apart. The propelling power is secured by the legs being brought from a position in which they are placed wide apart to one in which they are close together, like the blades of a pair of scissors. In this position the heels should touch each other; and in drawing up the legs, the toes should be pointed backward to avoid the resistance of the water against the insteps.

It may happen that you will swallow water in your first efforts; but this should not discourage you, neither should the fancy that because you make but little advance you are not capable of learning to swim. Every beginner has his mishaps, no matter what the art.

Some lads will learn to swim "dog-fashion" quicker than any other style; and while it is not at all graceful, it gradually leads into the smooth, even, scientific breast-stroke, and therefore should hardly be discouraged. Every boy, of course, knows that "dog-fashion" is that frantic motion of the hands and legs like a large paddle-wheel, in which more bluster and foam than headway are made; and every boy likes to swim "dog-fashion" occasionally, often just to "show off," or to imitate some friend not so far advanced as himself. But, "dog-fashion" swimmer, don't let such mimics dishearten you; keep right on, and soon you will master the breast-stroke as we have described it, and by studying some of the tricks in this article, you may soon have the laugh on your mockers.

Having mastered the breast-stroke, which is adapted to long-distance leisurely swimming, the next movement is the side-stroke; it may be the left or right, or either. You can accomplish it by shooting the right arm forward, while the left, like an oar, is forcing the water back, and the legs are propelling the body onward. This stroke, which is a powerful one, will move you on like clock-work, and for long distance moderately fast swimming is excellent.

Then follows the alternate right-hand, left-hand movement, or the overhand-stroke. This is perhaps the most graceful and convenient of all. In reaching forward, the arms are alternately brought out of the water, and then curved so that the tips of the fingers enter again directly in front of the head. This movement can be made very graceful by daintily skimming the palm along the surface, and merely dipping the water before it disappears. For short distance swimming, you will find no speedier stroke. Advancing the right and left sides of the body alternately, secures greater continuity of motion and materially reduces the friction; in conjunction with the powerful propulsion of the legs, it sends you along with the speed of a fish. As it is very swift, so it is very exhausting; it is, therefore, best adapted to racing, say fifty or one hundred yards.

I once saw Dennis F. Butler, the ex-champion of America, finish a seven-mile race against the tide with this overhand stroke; and he did it in a peculiar manner. With every dip of the arm his head would go under water; and thus he lolled, yet fairly plunged for the goal, taking breath every time he turned on his sides.

The boy aspirants to racing honors will do well to practise this movement diligently.

Back performances are more easily learned than those on the breast, and floating is quite simple.

Turn yourself over on your back, as gently as possible, elevate your breast above the surface, put your head back, so that your eyes, nose, and chin only are above water. Keep in this position with the arms and legs extended, the latter perfectly rigid. Now, move the hands from right to left horizontally, fast or slow as you choose, and you will find yourself buoyed up and gradually moving along. If you wish to make greater speed or swim on your back, begin to work your legs, precisely as in breast swimming, taking care not to lift the knees too high nor to sink your hips and sides too low. Keep yourself as straight as possible. You are now progressing finely — getting along easily and speedily. If your arms grow tired, lay them on your breast, but keep the legs going; thus you can rest your arms; if your legs tire, let them remain quiet, and renew work with your hands. Thus alternating, you will find yourself able to cover a long distance without fatigue.

Just at this stage of progress you will be anxious to dive. There is great sport in this; but it requires practice to dive " cleanly."

Diving may be performed from the surface of the water, when swimming, by merely turning the head downward, and striking upward with the legs. It is, however, much better to leap in, with the hands closed above the head, and the head foremost, from a pier, boat, or raised bank. The proper attitude for a " clean " dive — which means without splashing more than the sharp cut of the hands — is to place the hands over the head, close together, give a sudden spring, and descend through the air, heels together and body perfectly stiff. Your hands will cleave the way for your body, protecting your head, and you will pass beneath the surface just like the inimitable bull-frog — the master-diver.

By striking with the feet, the same as in swimming, and keeping the head toward the bottom, you can drive yourself to a considerable depth.

If you wish to reach the surface, turn your head upward and work your hands, up and down; you will ascend like a flash.

To turn under water, merely swim in whichever direction you wish.

Some swimmers prefer to keep their eyes open while beneath the surface; I do not consider it wise, as the strain is great, and often foreign substances in the water are liable to injure the eyeball. Of course, if you dive for an object at the bottom, you will need to open your eyes to find it; at other times I advise you to keep them closed.

Swimming under water is accomplished by the ordinary stroke, but take care to keep your head a little downward and strike a little higher with your feet than when swimming on the surface.

Perhaps as easy a way as any of learning to swim under water is by beginning, in shallow water, to simply sink below the surface of the water. This

*The Diver.*

can be done by letting the air escape from the lungs, so that they lose their power of buoyancy. The beginner, having no fear of being unable to reach *terra firma*, will learn far quicker in this way to be at home beneath the surface than if he attempts to swim at the outset. When once confidence is gained, all that remains is to learn the trick of staying below the surface when the lungs are inflated.

If you have successfully practised these lessons, you are familiar with the three essential elements of swimming, and in prime condition to study a few tricks.

"Treading water" is a fine feat. To tread without the use of the hands, work your feet up and down, precisely as though ascending a flight of stairs, only with more speed and steadiness. You will find this very simple, and oftentimes you can stand where the water is a fathom deep and by treading hold the hands high over the head, and make the uninitiated suppose you to be on the bottom. In this position, also, you can walk a considerable distance, when you are expert. If you want to ease your legs, put your arms under, and work them horizontally right and left, as in floating.

The feat of breast-swimming without the use of

hands requires strength in the legs and back. At best, but a short distance can be made in this way. The same may be said of swimming without the use of the legs. But it is well to practise both of these movements — they may save your life in the event of cramp or accident.

To show the feet while floating, bend the small of the back downward, support yourself by moving your hands to and fro just above your breast, and stretch your feet above the water. Now, if you wish to swim on your back, feet-foremost, make precisely the same stroke as in breast-swimming.

To swim with one hand out of the water, say the right, turn on the left side, and vigorously use that arm, and the legs.

If you wish to turn while on your back, keep one leg still, and embrace the water beside you with the other; you will thus find yourself turning to that side on which your leg by its motion embraces the water, and you will turn to the right or left according to which leg you use in this manner.

There are a variety of feats performed by expert swimmers; such as floating on the back with the arms above the surface; taking the left leg in the right hand out of the water when swimming on the back; pulling the right heel by the right hand toward the back, when swimming in the common way; throwing somersaults in the water, backward and forward, etc., for which no particular directions are necessary, as you will be able to do them and any tricks which your fancy may suggest.

A few hygienic hints for swimmers will surely not be out of place here.

Do not bathe too soon after eating; an interval of an hour and a half at least, should be allowed. Do not bathe when tired out, either mentally or physically — always wait till you feel rested. The best time for this exercise is in the forenoon, between breakfast and luncheon.

If overheated on arriving at the water, do not remove your clothes until the excessive feeling of heat has passed, and your breathing and circulation have become regular; never expose the skin to the direct action of the air when overheated.

Keep in motion after you have gone into the water; do not stand around chatting and lounging. As soon as you have swum sufficiently, dry yourself thoroughly, put on your clothes, and keep the blood in circulation by exercise.

Do not stay in the water too long — half an hour

is long enough for the strongest man. More delicate persons will find that too much; for some, ten minutes should be the limit. Fifteen minutes is a good average for all.

If seized with cramp, endeavor not to be alarmed, but strike out vigorously with the affected limb, or, turning on the back, extend it forcibly into the air. By paddling with the hands you can easily reach shore, or keep afloat until assistance is rendered.

And, never, never "duck" your weaker brother! The poor fellow might take fright, and never again essay to learn; besides, you might accidentally drown him.

In conclusion: if you have followed these suggestions, not merely mentally, but in the "aqueous element," as the student would say, you will have become dexterous swimmers, and soon shall be able to join Byron in this stanza: —

> "How many a time have I
> Cloven with an arm still lustier, breast more daring,
> The wave all roughen'd; with a swimmer's stroke
> Flinging the billows back from my drench'd hair,
> And, laughing, from my lip the audacious brine,
> Which kiss'd it, like a wine-cup, rising o'er
> The waves as they arose, and prouder still
> The loftier they uplifted me."

# SPORT IN THE WATER.

### BY ALEXANDER BLACK.

ANY one who has ever seen a tub race — and those who have not may be assured that they have missed one of the funniest sights in the world — will remember the screams of laughter and little shrieks of momentary fear that come from the spectators when the first conspicuous tub turns wrong side up, and dumps its occupant head-first into the water. For the moment, it seems to those of the audience who are unskilled in swimming as if the overturned racer were certain to drown. But very soon his head pops up through the foam, the tub is righted, and, if the racer is skilful, the uncertain craft is manned again. By and by the spectators begin to realize, if they never have before, that there is really no danger that any one will drown, and every new mishap brings more laughter and fewer sounds of fright.

In fact, while it is easy for everybody to think of sport on the water, a comparatively small number are able to fully appreciate the idea of sport in the water. The seaside bather cannot be said to know what water sport means; for the seaside bather, in the great majority of cases, does not know how to swim. Only those who know how to swim can really know what water sport is; for only these can know what it is to be free, safe, and "at home" in the water.

Probably water sports are as old as any other kind of sports. The very fish in the depths of the lake, in the shallows of the brook, or in the clear green depths of the sea, are continually giving a hint of the gayety that is to be found in the water. Life under water has many amusements. Seals have set games that they romp in, day after day, when the weather is inviting. Naturalists tell wonderful stories of the fishes and of those animals who can get along very comfortably both in and out of the water. And does anybody suppose that the boys of antiquity did not follow the sportive example of the light-hearted frog?

Among wild people living near any sort of deep water, there have always been water games. Indian boys were experts in various contests and festivals in the water, and some of the South Sea Island boys seem to get along about as well in the water as out of it.

**Winning the Tub-Race.**

Tub-racing, which is a very old sport, is to be classed with sports in the water, like swimming, rather than with sports on the water, like rowing or sailing; for it is understood that the tubs turn over a good deal, and that cleverness at swimming and manœuvring in the water will come into play. And of course tub-racing gets its main excitement and fun not so much from the mere progress of the tubs as from the continual chance of accident — that is, the comical accident of the racer's plunge into the water.

Somebody who understood how much delight was to be had from the make-believe danger of this kind of accident, as well as from other absurd intentional blunders, invented the modern water circus. For there is such a thing as a water circus, a circus with a ring — but a ring of water instead of sawdust.

Away back in the old Roman days the water circus was a wonderful affair. Arenas would be flooded, and naval battles would be fought between great galleys for the amusement of the emperor and the people. Things are not on quite so vast or serious a scale now, however; and the water circus, as it is seen in Europe to-day, is but one of the features of an ordinary circus. But, the American reader will ask, how can a water circus be part of an ordinary circus? Can they flood the ring? And even if they did, would it be deep enough for any kind of water sport? The fact is, that they do not flood an ordinary ring, which would not hold more than an ankle-deep puddle; but this is the way it is done: —

When that point in the circus programme that is set for the beginning of the water show has been successfully reached, a small army of clowns and "supers" begin dragging into the arena sections of an iron tank, which, amid much ludicrous play on the part of the clowns, is fitted together in the ring, before the eyes of the amused and expectant audience. The pieces lock tightly together, and a huge roll of rubber that is tumbled into the circle with many comical struggles and mishaps, is spread out to make the bottom of the lake thoroughly water-tight. When this has been done, a bridge, generally with a double arch and a central platform, which has been suspended overhead with the trapeze bars and other circus paraphernalia, is lowered to the little lake and duly fits into its place.

On one side of the ring — now the lake — a series of embankments rise to the musicians' gallery. At the proper moment, generally when the attention of the audience is directed to the final preparations in the circle below, there is a gush of water from under the gallery, and a fine cascade splashes its way over the embankments down to the now completed tank. Generally somebody screams at the first roar of the water; then everybody joins in shouts and stampings of applause at the sight of the waterfall, which dances and sparkles and splutters in the rays of the electric light. The cascade is, indeed, one of the great features of the show; for the electric glare changes in hue, until the bubbling torrent, from seeming like a flood of very green sea-water, turns to a crimson and then to a golden shower, and is once more foaming white again.

And then, while the water is splashing, and the people are laughing and chattering, and the band is performing with great energy, the clowns toss several screaming ducks into the lake, which is, of course, in a very turbulent state, and gives the ducks a good deal to do for a little while. Very soon, however, the ducks make themselves at home, and the spectators take as much interest in seeing the fowl swim about as if the sight really were very novel indeed.

When once the tank is quite filled, a decided change comes over the scene. A skiff containing a young man and a young woman — who is much afraid of the water — makes its appearance, the young man rowing with an air of conscious ele-

At the Water Circus.— The Fat Policeman as a Life-preserver.

gance and dexterity. A group of dancers comes skipping over the bridge to the jaunty strains of the band. Various picturesque promenaders follow the dancers. Then a delightfully solemn, matter-of-fact squire makes his appearance, fishing-pole in hand, and casts a line with every sign of lively expectancy. Presently he has a most extraordinary bite, one of those bites that you read about in the fish-story column of the newspaper. The squire, amusingly bewildered, tugs at the pole, and raises what seems to be a tremendous fish, whose struggles spatter the occupants of the skiff, and completely destroy the self-possession of the squire.

While things are at this crisis, the spirit of mischief seems to break loose. Some mischief-makers who appear on the bridge complete the squire's anxiety by knocking his hat into the water; and very soon the fisherman himself manages to tumble in, pole, line, fish, and all. A country woman with a basket, who is solicitous about the squire's fate, falls with a great splash, and so does a dude, who has been shocked to discover that his shoes are wet. Matters are considerably jumbled in this way when a policeman appears on the scene. The policeman wears beneath his uniform a rubber suit which has been inflated to a wonderful size. He wobbles upon the bridge, looking about with great concern and indignation, asking what all this means. In his efforts to restore order or rescue somebody, he shares the fate of the others, bouncing into the lake in a manner so absurd as to excite fresh screams of laughter from the audience. The people in the water, discovering how buoyant the fat policeman is, at once seize upon him as a life-preserver, and the dude actually clambers astride of the portly figure, while the spectators laugh until the tears come. When the skiff has been overturned, and everything in the water is in a state of the liveliest confusion, a great spurt of water rises through the centre of the bridge, the spray of the sudden and graceful fountain is lighted by flashes of colored fire, and the water circus is at an end.

I think it will appear to be quite natural that the water circus should be very popular. It has already appeared in this country, though not to the extent it has been given in Europe. It will probably become more popular with us as time goes on, though perhaps an entertainment in which so many actors have to run the risk of colds and rheumatism may not be considered very promising in our climate.

But if this should be an objection, why is it that the latest and most popular of our water games is played almost wholly in winter? I am speaking of water polo, which within a few years has been growing in favor, until it is now one of the most cordially welcomed of all our sports. Temperature has, of course, a great deal to do with a game that is pursued in the costume of the swimmer. In the swimming-tanks of athletic clubs or gymnasiums, the temperature of the water can be regulated, and the temperature of the air can be brought up to the warmth of what has been called the "Turkish bath" atmosphere. There is no reason why the

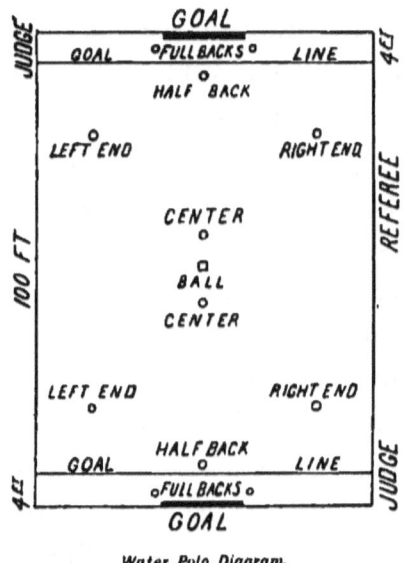

Water Polo Diagram.

same conditions cannot be supplied in summer, when the air is naturally warm, and the water in a tank, without artificial heating, would soon be sufficiently warm. Undoubtedly there has been, hitherto, little water polo in summer, because in the warm season out-door sports of another kind tempt the athlete. Lake, river, and deep-sea swimming lure him away from the narrow dimensions of a tank. But as water polo gains in popularity, and begins to take rank as something more than a game to be played in-doors and in winter, when other forms of athletic sports are comparatively inaccessible, it is less likely to be set aside in the summer season. Indeed, water polo is continually on the increase as a summer sport.

Our American water polo is simply foot-ball played in the water. It might seem more out of place to use the term foot-ball in a water game which does not permit the kicking of the ball, if modern foot-ball had not done away with a great deal of the kicking that once seemed the special characteristic of the game. The fact that foot-ball has, paradoxically, become so much of a hand game, makes it much more feasible than it once might have been to transfer the game to the water.

Water polo is not yet an exact science, either as regards the manner of the game or the place where it is played. There is much difference of opinion as to the proper size of the tank in which it should be played. Some players hold to a deep tank, in which everybody would have to swim throughout the game. Others are much in favor of a tank with a uniform depth of five feet or thereabouts, so that the player could stand when swimming was not demanded. Most of the games thus far have been played in the regular athletic club tanks. These are four or five feet deep at one end, and increase in depth toward the other end, until there they hold six feet or more of water. Unless special water polo tanks are constructed, in-door games will probably continue to be played in the tanks that are comparatively shallow at one end — although four feet of water is not to be despised in the opportunities it gives the swimmer.

A water polo team consists of six men, who are organized on the same general plan as a foot-ball team. Thus, there is a centre rush, two end rushers, a half-back, and two full backs or goal keepers. The accompanying diagram will give an idea of the way the team ranges itself in the water. The goal boards are about four feet long and twelve inches wide, and on each is painted the word "Goal" in large letters. The boards are about eighteen inches above the water-line. The goal line indicated on the diagram is an imaginary line, running between two marks on the sides of the tank, four feet from the end. The tank we shall suppose to be one hundred feet long and twenty feet wide. As the side with the shallower end has somewhat of an advantage, choice of end is decided by toss at the beginning of the game, and the sides alternate in position.

Only the full backs or goal keepers are entitled to remain within the goal-line; and it is one of the duties of the judges or umpires, who stand each at a goal, to declare a foul against any player who enters the goal enclosure ahead of the ball. It is one of the rules, too, that the ball must be carried, and cannot be passed, over the goal-line.

There are several points of difference between the English and the American game. In the English game, as I understand, the player is permitted to strike or push the ball with his hand. He may interfere with an opponent only when the opponent has the ball in his possession. In this country a player may carry the ball in any direction, and may "tackle" any player who either has the ball or is within three feet of it.

At the moment before the beginning of the game the teams are marshalled on the platforms, at the respective ends of the tank, as determined by the toss. It is a moment of expectancy. The twelve young men in their swimming costumes make two attractive groups. The ball, ready for its lively bath, is the regulation foot-ball. The umpires, timekeeper, referee, are all in place. The audience gives signs of that tension exhibited at the moment in foot-ball when the two teams, drawn up in determined lines, await that first movement of the ball which begins the excitement of the game.

"Go!"

The ball is in the middle of the tank, and with a great splash the players are plunging into the water. The two centre rushes are swimming toward the ball from opposite sides of the tank, the other players scurrying into position behind them. For a few seconds only there is the suspense of not knowing which leader will first get the ball. Almost at the same instant the Red and the Black reach for the dancing globe. But the Red gets it; and quick as thought he snaps it to the half-back, the end

*The Struggle for the Ball.*

rusher continuing to plunge toward the opposite goal. The half-back, clutching the ball, dives out of sight for an instant, but is soon seen on his way toward the left centre of the tank. The centre rush of the Blacks makes a great sweeping stroke for the ball, and the left end rusher of the Blacks is right in the swimmer's path. There is a big fluster of spray, and the left end rusher of the Reds is seen swimming with the ball that was cleverly passed to him. But the half-back of the enemy is alert, and by a swift side-stroke wrenches the ball from the daring rusher, and makes for the other side of the tank. Here two of his team make a lively effort to keep a passage for him. Five swimmers are soon in such a tangle that it is difficult to determine who has the ball. Three or four of the figures disappear beneath the foam; and one man, another of the Blacks, is seen swimming hard for the Red goal.

There is a great cheer from the spectators as the lusty youth cleaves the water with his free left arm. But the swimmer can gain but a few strokes. He is seized by two of the Reds; he writhes, dives, and appears two yards away, rising, unfortunately, under the very nose of the Red left end rusher, who has waited for him. Two other Reds are but a stroke or two away, and all of them disappear and rise again. The head of the Black with the ball cannot be seen by the eager spectators. They are holding him under. Yet he seems determined not to give up the ball. Re-enforcements from both teams are now at hand. Two of the Blacks dive with the purpose of passing the ball. But a man with his head under water and three or four men struggling with him cannot discriminate very readily in such a matter. The plucky fellow, who cannot tell whose hand is friendly, must soon let go the ball, and who shall get it when he does let go?

Then all at once two of the players who have been on the outskirts of the struggle discover that the ball has come to the surface a yard away from the outer line of the scramble. A Red now has the ball. He is making straight for the right of the tank. The crowd of swimmers turn upon him. A signal has told the Reds that the ball is in their possession. Three times the glistening rubber changes hands, the Reds still carrying it nearer and nearer to their opponents' goal. The Black goal keepers gird themselves for the struggle beyond the goal line. Twice the Blacks get the ball. Twice the

Reds recover it. The spectators are finding it hard not to shout improperly loud, and not to stand on the seats. The shouts in the water often end in a gurgle, and a seething hum is punctuated with an occasional splash on the surface.

In the scramble at the goal-line it is again impossible to tell who has the ball, but the Reds are holding all the ground (or water) they have taken. The effort is to touch the goal-board. This is no easy thing in the presence of two goal-keepers with arms like a blacksmith's. The water is white with foam, and every swimmer is doing his utmost to turn the crisis to the advantage of his side. When the referee's whistle announces that the Reds have won the goal, a congratulatory shout greets the panting and dripping figures that leave the water for a few minutes' breathing-time.

Enthusiasts in water polo think that before the present summer is over the game will be established in favor as a warm-weather sport. There is, these enthusiasts tell me, no reason in the world why the game should not be played in any water that is without current; and, even in a river with moderately strong current, it would be possible to play it across stream, the goals and limits being once definitely placed. Probably, however, the popularity of the game will result in the arrangement of warm weather arenas for the sport, where everything can be done scientifically and in order. I think it has been suggested that there is a good deal of "science" in water polo. While the game is being studied out, there will be a good deal of roughness. But this roughness will in great measure diminish as skill and precision are acquired.

Whatever may become of water polo, the new sport has certainly given a great "boom" to swimming. All athletics in the water are based on the swimmer's art; and when swimming is surrounded by proper precautions against accident, it is one of the most healthful forms of exercise, encouraging muscular self-confidence, strengthening the frame, and building up the lungs. There will always, I suppose, be differences of opinion as to the best kind of stroke. The "overhand" stroke is fast for a short distance; the English "side stroke" is highly praised, and is practised by many prize winners. But the old-fashioned "breast stroke" is not likely to go out of fashion for a long while.

I suppose that in that interesting future we all like to talk about we shall have some surprising devices for travelling as well as amusing ourselves in water. We already have the water bicycle. Captain Boynton's water-shoes sound better than they look, and I fancy that they look better than they feel. As might be imagined from their appearance,

*The Water Shoes.*

these water-shoes do not permit a seven-league stride; in fact, they do not permit striding at all. You simply have a boat on each foot, and must get yourself along with an oar or some other means of propulsion. If a person were in a hurry, it would pay to get these shoes off and swim. Captain

Boynton's floating-suit was better, because it did not give so good an opportunity for getting the head under water and keeping it there. With an umbrella up to keep off the sun, a little floating box of provisions and utensils, and a neat paddle, Captain Boynton was really ready for a long and safe water journey.

But the ability to swim well, and for a long distance if necessary, is worth all the water apparatus that will ever be invented.

# A CANE RUSH.

### BY MALCOLM TOWNSEND.

DID you ever see a "cane rush"? It is not altogether new; for when the Greek boys of the Twenty-third Olympiad — twenty-five hundred years and more ago — tugged and struggled for the mastery in the game of strength and muscle known to them as the *pancratium*, they were but striving for the prize of the wild olive wreath in a rough and tumble game which, centuries later, was to reappear in what is known in certain American colleges as the "cane rush."

All athletic sports have in them a certain element of danger; all of them, pushed to extremes, may degenerate into brutality. The deadly pitching of the base-ball field, the "slugging" of many a football match, have again and again brought discredit upon those noble tests of strength and skill. But the gentleman cannot be a brute; and if but the demands of courtesy and manliness are kept ever in view, no field sport, however exciting, however risky, or however absorbing, need ever pass that border line that separates chivalry from brutishness.

A cane rush may be reduced to a brutal level, and become dangerous to the participants. But when planned upon a manly athletic basis, and controlled by the spirit of friendly rivalry, it is, perhaps, one of the most exciting contests adopted by the restless college "men." When participated in along the lines of courtesy and courage, it enlists a Spartan element of honor. It is regarded as a duty which no loyal class member would think of shirking. It cements a class union that otherwise would never be formed, enthusiastically contributed to by the many secret meetings, private conferences, and careful "pointers" that precede the day of contest.

Let me describe for you a cane rush in a certain college, where brutality is frowned down, and the boys can be gentlemen even in the heat of conflict.

It is the battle for supremacy between Sophomores and Freshmen — the class of '94 and the class of '95. And the sign of supremacy, to be borne away by the victors, is the conquered cane.

The time at last has arrived — a cool fall day. The combatants are full of pluck and determination. After class hours the rendezvous of the collegians is the green field not far away — a piece of turf still famous as the scene of a deadly encounter between two rival American statesmen.

The field is thronged with spectators. Here are representatives of the alumni, the professors, the friends, the brothers, the fathers, and a goodly sprinkling even of gray-haired grandfathers.

The Sophomores have had the advantage of experience. The year preceding they, as Freshmen, fought the "Sophs" — the Juniors of to-day. This apparent disadvantage under which the Freshmen enter the contest generally turns the sympathy of the spectator to them, so that they become the centre of attraction, being the new blood of the contest.

The arena, or battle-ground, is a rectangular plot

one hundred feet in length, with its outer lines marked and guarded by stakes and rope. A well-sodded part of the field is generally chosen. Across the centre of the enclosure a chalk-line is drawn. The cane is a strong, smooth, rounded stick, about five feet in length, and from an inch and a half to two inches in diameter.

Judges chosen from the alumni are detailed to see that neither kicking nor striking an opponent takes place; they are also to decide the final count of hands remaining on the cane at the call of "time." A "hand" is three fingers, or two fingers and the thumb; both hands of one party on the cane is counted as two hands. A kick or blow decided against a class member is a forfeit of "one hand" at the final count — a serious penalty.

Signals are given by pistol-shots from the starter: first shot, "make ready;" second shot, "charge;" third shot, "withdraw." Five minutes is allowed between the second and the third shot.

The contestants are the Sophomores and the Freshmen; the former are the challengers.

The men are divided into five sections for special work: the Gladiatoræ, or centres, who hold the cane; the Robustæ, or strongest men; the Avelli, or "pullers;" the Salturæ, or "jumpers;" and the Palæstræ, or "wrestlers."

"Time is up!" announces the starter. Out from the dressing-room of the club-house come the challengers, the "class of '94," marching under the

The Gladiatoriæ Holding the Cane.

leadership of its captain, who ranges his men at the northerly line of the arena, forming his line with the strength in the centre, and graduating it down to the "light weights" at the extreme ends. The "class of '95" next marches out, and in similar

230   THE BOOK OF ATHLETICS.

manner is lined up at the extreme south end, ranged according to strength.

The costume donned for the fray presents a gladiatorial effect; every man is stripped to the waist; the exposed parts have been rubbed thick

*The Palestræ Wrestling for Time.*

with vaseline to produce a slippery surface that a grip will not hold. The palms of the hands are heavily coated with resin to overcome, in a measure, the greased skin. Out from under the greasy gloss is outlined in yellow, on the chest and back, the class number, " '94 " or " '95," marked large and distinctly with iodine. It is a "flesh-mark" of identification, as class members are not always recognizable. The heaviest and strongest of trousers are worn buckled tightly around the waist by inside strapping, twine lashing the trousers at the feet around well-greased strong shoes that will not break. Every means is adopted to prevent the advantage of obtaining a "hold."

First shot: "Make ready."

The "centres," two of the strongest men from each class, take a position on each side of the chalk line. The cane, after examination, is handed them by one of the judges; immediately the eight hands twist and slide around its surface to get a lasting grip.

Then the class "yell" goes up from the contestants, who now drop into a foot-racer's position and await the word "go!" Each man sights the cane and their "stalwarts" who are holding it, and inwardly vows to do his best.

Second shot: "Charge!"

And a hundred young men cover the distance of fifty feet in a twinkling, and come together with a crash and crush, taking down to the ground, almost unseen, the "centres," burying them three to four deep — each "unseen" reaching desperately, straining every muscle to wedge his hands down to the cane and maintain a grip.

Appearing like some immense octopus whose tentacles are human legs, this live mass of humanity surges, oscillates, wriggles, writhes, and struggles. Around its outer edge the "pullers" are active, as they reach into the pile and grab a leg or legs, and with a "long pull and a strong pull" drag out a powerless wight, and fling him out into the field, where the "wrestlers" interlock and down him, keeping their hold to the last. The outer field is besprinkled with these wrestlers, each with his man in tight embrace — a realistic representation of the dead gladiators of the Coliseum, for in fact dead they are to a chance of having a "hand" on the cane.

The squirming mass, head rubbing head, keeps up its straining; the "pullers" still haul out their victims and lessen the pile. Then new muscle enters the contest. With a run and spring high over the mass, headlong down into the central pit of heads, dive the "fliers," and working their way through by squeezing out the most exhausted, thrust their hands to a fresh hold of the coveted cane.

The Supreme Struggle in the Centre.

"Three-quarters of a minute yet," remarks a by-stander. It has seemed an age since that last shot. Not a word is heard from the strugglers; there is a bottling of all the reserve air in the lungs. Grunts and puffs are the only exhibit of breathings; the centre fairly steams from the perspiring mass.

Bang! the third shot.

The struggle ceases and the living mound dissolves; the upper tier is disentangled, the second strata backs off carefully, the third layer is rolled off, and then the judges, demanding stillness, note the names of the victors who hold the "mark of three" that counts for his class. Swathed with perspiration and dirt, with back tatooed by scratches of button or shoe, and face etched with finger-nail or pebble, one by one the rushers are picked up and led to quarters, proudly passing inspection, and displaying their battle scars and ragged raiment.

The judges announce the score. It stands, "thirteen hands for '94," and "sixteen hands for '95." The crowd shouts its approval; loud and strong is given the class yell of '95; and '93 (the Juniors), who back the winners, echo the Fresh yell with their own.

It is the first victory for a Freshman class in the history of the college.

The victory gives the privilege to the Freshmen to carry a cane for a year, and denies it to the Sophomores for the same period. The buttonhole in the lapel of the coat of each Freshman the next morning sarcastically carries to class a miniature

*'Ninety-fiive !*

cane, and each man expresses a desire to see a Soph walking with a cane, that he can exercise his battle-won privilege of breaking it.

When the next fall comes around, the Freshman of to-day becomes the "Soph" of to-morrow, and must again fight over the cane to maintain the supremacy he has won. A rough and tumble game, do you say? I grant it; but, as I said at the outset, a cane rush, when "rushed" by young gentlemen who can keep their heads cool and their hearts friendly, however may go the day, is able to be carried out, from start to finish, along the lines of courtesy and courage.

# HURDLING.

### BY HERBERT MAPES.*

*Intercollegiate Champion at the High Hurdles, 1888-89.*

EXCEPT among athletes and college men, interest in the minor athletic sports is, comparatively, confined to so few people that it would not be strange if many young Americans had never seen, nor even heard of, a hurdle race. Hence, perhaps, it is advisable to begin by briefly describing one.

As the name implies, the race is run over hurdles. The hurdle is of wood, and consists of two uprights and a cross-bar. This cross-bar is either two feet

---

* Herbert Mapes, of the class of 1890 in Columbia College, was drowned while bathing in the surf at Fire Island, in the summer of 1891. He was a young man of rare promise, distinguished in his college, and much beloved by his classmates and a wide circle of friends. His record for scholarship and in athletics was equally high, and his work at the hurdles was almost phenomenal. This article on hurdling, written by him, is here reprinted by permission of his father, Mr. Charles V. Mapes, and of the *St. Nicholas* magazine, in which the article originally appeared.

six inches or three feet six inches from the ground, according to the distance to be run. The longer of the two distances commonly run by hurdlers is two hundred and twenty yards, and for this the hurdles are two feet six inches high; the shorter distance is one hundred and twenty yards, with the hurdles three feet six inches high. There are generally ten hurdles, which are set across a track, or path, made either of fine cinders or of turf. When arranged for the race, these ten hurdles are technically known as a "flight." The contestants are drawn up in a line a few yards from the first hurdle, and at a given signal they run and jump each hurdle in succession, the one who first reaches the finish-line being the winner.

Now, hurdling, being merely a combination of running and jumping, might appear to require no special ability. Some people foolishly believe that any boy who has long legs must be a fast runner; and, more reasonably, those of better judgment might be led to infer that a good runner and jumper must necessarily be a good hurdler. But experience has shown that this is not the case. Not every good runner and jumper makes a good hurdler; and, strangely enough, some of the most

The Finish of an Intercollegiate Hurdle Race. (From an instantaneous photograph by A. H. Mosely, of Yale.)

celebrated hurdlers have been neither very fast runners nor exceptionally good jumpers. For, besides skill in running and jumping, other qualities are necessary; and it is in these that the true genius for hurdling seems to lie. Without special skill, which can come only after long practice, success in hurdling is not to be attained.

It is difficult with few words to make clear in just what this skill consists, or why so much practice is necessary. Perhaps the best way to explain matters is to indicate some of the difficulties that appear before the new hurdler when he begins his training. Suppose, for instance, he is training for the shorter race of a hundred and twenty yards, where the hurdles are three feet and six inches high, and are set ten yards apart.

Like all other athletes, the hurdler must undergo a regular course of training in order to acquire strength and endurance; but from the very beginning he concentrates his attention more especially upon his "style." The first particular to be considered is, naturally, the manner of jumping over the hurdle. As the race is one of speed, it is of great importance for him to learn to clear the hurdles with as little room to spare as possible.

He must learn to "take" the hurdle without changing his stride or stopping his speed,— in such a way that jumping the hurdle comes as near as possible to *running* over the hurdle. With this end in view, he sets up a single hurdle and betakes himself to practising the jump. When in this he has succeeded to his satisfaction, he sets up two hurdles, and practises taking them in succession. And here a new and very important question arises.

The hurdles are ten yards apart ; and after he has jumped the first and run to the second, he very often finds himself coming before it with his wrong foot foremost. In order to jump, he must slacken his pace and change his stride. Here is a difficulty. He must devise some way of jumping the hurdles in succession without hesitating between them. There are two or three methods of doing this, though one method has come to be regarded as the right one.

In the first place, he may practise jumping from the wrong or awkward foot, and so be prepared to jump in whichever way he may come to the hurdle. But the hurdles are too high to make this plan practicable, and it is generally abandoned after a few days' trial. (It is, however, only in the shorter race that the hurdles are so high as to prevent this method from being successful. The low hurdles, two feet six inches high, used for the longer race, have been jumped from alternate feet with notable success by A. F. Copeland, the American champion.)

With the high hurdles there is but one good method. A hurdler must either shorten his natural stride and learn to take five steps beween hurdles, or he must lengthen it considerably and take only three. In either case he is brought to the successive hurdles with the same foot. But taking five steps makes the stride too short to allow of fast running; and, although many of the poorer hurdlers have used this method, it cannot be regarded as successful. So there is nothing for the hurdler to do but continually to practise taking three long strides, until this becomes natural to him.

Even when the hurdler has learned to jump low and fast, and to take three strides between the hurdles, the development of "style" is hardly more than begun. There are a thousand and one requirements in the turn and twist used in the jump; and it is in the methods of taking the hurdle that the marked differences between advanced hurdlers are shown. Here the individuality of each hurdler asserts itself. After he has attained a certain degree of proficiency, his attention is confined almost wholly to perfecting his "turn," the aim always being to clear the hurdle as closely as possible without interfering with speed or stride

This, as might be supposed, leads to frequent accidents, and is the chief source of danger in hurdling. In his anxiety to take the hurdle closely, the hurdler sometimes jumps too low and strikes the hurdle; the result in many cases being a heavy fall on the cinder-path. But it takes a strong knock to tumble, or even to stagger, an experienced hurdler. Indeed, the best hurdlers have been known to win races in which they struck nearly every hurdle, and even knocked down a number as they went along.

A. A. Jordan, the celebrated hurdler of the New York Athletic Club, contracted the habit of striking hurdles to an extreme degree. Yet this did not seem to interfere in the least with his success; nor did it mar the beauty of his style, which was perhaps better than that of any hurdler who had then appeared in America. He was the first exponent

*Hurdling on Skates in Canada.*

of the peculiar finished style that has been adopted by so many leading hurdlers of to-day; and, indeed, he might perhaps be called the "Father of American Hurdling." He and Copeland of the Manhattan Athletic Club were at one time the best-known hurdlers in America, and their struggles for supremacy have been hard-fought and brilliant.

After a hurdler has perfected his style, and is in the pink of condition, all ready for the race, there is no prettier sight on the athletic field than to see him taking a practice-spin over the whole flight of hurdles. True and strong in his motions, running and jumping with all his might, he yet rises and falls lightly as a bird, handling himself so gracefully withal, that, to a mere observer, the sport appears to be without difficulty.

The real question of supremacy each year concerns only three or four hurdlers, who make the great championship struggle. All the others can expect only lesser honors, though always there are many who have secret hopes of improving sufficiently to enter the first rank. In order to provide opportunity and incentive for the mass of athletes of no special distinction, numerous handicap races are held, in which the different competitors are allowed starts according to their supposed abilities. Of course there is no great interest at stake in these games beyond the individual desire to win. Even for the novice the honor of victory is much diminished on account of the handicap in his favor; and among athletes the winning or losing in such cases is considered of less importance than the merit of the performances. But for all that, there is always a certain satisfaction in being victorious; and the prizes given, in themselves, make success worth striving for.

From this fact there is quite a large class of athletes, called "mug-hunters," who have no further ambition than to win as many of these handicap games as possible. As it is essential to their success that they should have big handicaps, they use every means to conceal their true ability, whatever it may be, and always take pains to win a race by no more than is absolutely necessary. Fortunately, however, such athletes are hardly more than tolerated; and the name "mug-hunter" has come to be used as a term of reproach.

A handicap hurdle-race, although there are no great interests at stake, is a very pretty sight. When the contestants take their positions for the race, it looks like a hopeless struggle for the "scratch" man (that is, the one who stands farthest back of all the contestants, and who allows "starts" to all the others. He is called the "scratch" man because he toes the "scratch," or line, at the beginning of the course). Often he is small in stature, as is Copeland, for instance; and when he stands there with the other contestants, many of them larger and stronger than he, and some of them ten or fifteen yards in advance of him, the arrangement appears altogether unfair, and the spectator, who is likely to regard the "scratch" man's chance as hopeless, is filled with sympathy for him. When all is ready, the starter calls out, "On your marks!" All stand upright in their positions. "Settle." They all lean forward, ready for the start. "Bang!" goes the pistol, and they are off! The leaders are almost to the second hurdle before the "scratch" man reaches the first; it seems impossible that he should overtake them. But now see skill and speed tell. While they rush and jump clumsily and high, lumbering along with all their might, truly and prettily he skims the hurdles and flies over the ground. Yet the handicap seems too large, and they are three-quarters through the race before he has had time

The "Scratch" Man at the Finish.

even to close up the gap between himself and the man nearest him. As they draw closer to the finish, his speed seems to increase; and he shoots by them one by one, until, when the last hurdle is reached, he is abreast of the leader. Then with a burst of speed he rushes for the tape, and wins the race!

Of course the "scratch" man does not always win; but if he is in his best condition, he is not likely to be beaten. At all events he is sure to give a fine exhibition, because to be "scratch" he must be a good hurdler, and often he is the champion.

Far greater, however, in real interest than any handicap event are the great "scratch" races of the year, the amateur championships and the intercollegiates, where only the best of amateur and college hurdlers compete, and all start even. The intercollegiate contests are, perhaps, even more exciting than the championships, because college rivalries, as well as those of friends and contestants, are concerned in the result. For some five months each representative has been faithfully training in preparation for the great race that lasts only a few seconds. A single misstep, and he feels that all the work goes for nothing; his college may lose the cup, and there is a year's disappointment before him.

It is no wonder that the boys are nervous as they take their places and wait for the start. But when once the signal is given and they are off, all is forgotten; the race has begun, and every one flies over the hurdles, conscious only that the supreme moment has come, and that he is rushing on for victory.

# THE RUNNING BROAD JUMP.

### BY E. B. BLOSS,
#### *Intercollegiate Champion of* 1892-93.

IN explaining my method of broad jumping, I think I can arrive at greater clearness by dividing the subject into several parts, and treating the reader as one entirely unacquainted with the sport.

In the first place, it is very necessary for the athlete to go to work systematically; otherwise it will be impossible to attain satisfactory results. He should, first of all, find out where his "marks" come. He can do this by starting at the farther end of the jumping-path, and running toward the take-off at the top of his speed. It will be only after repeated trials that his jumping-foot will strike the take-off exactly. Having succeeded in this, let him trace back his strides, and, at a convenient distance from the take-off, make his first or front mark. The number of strides should be determined by the athlete himself, who knows best how much ground he must cover before he gets up his greatest speed. I am in the habit of counting back nine strides, which is just fifty-nine feet from the take-off. Suppose the athlete counts back this number. At the point where the ninth stride comes, let him make a mark along the running-path; then from this mark count back about a dozen more strides, and make a second mark. Now he has his two marks, and can feel reasonably sure that if he starts from the second, strikes the front mark squarely with his jumping-foot, and then runs nine strides at the top of his speed, he will hit his take-off exactly and make a good jump. Various conditions, however, may alter somewhat the position of this front mark. If the wind happens to be blowing noticeably in the athlete's face or on his back, it will have the effect, respectively, of shortening or of lengthening his stride, and the mark should be moved accordingly. Again, the fact that the running-path has just been rolled hard, or chances to be wet and heavy, should also cause the position of the mark to be altered. Neglect to attend to these seeming trifles may spoil the athlete's run, and prevent him from doing himself justice.

Next let us learn how to run up to the take-off properly. The athlete, having started with his right foot on the second mark, should run toward his front mark at such a rate of speed that he will neither fall short of striking it, nor go over it altogether. If he fails to strike his front mark fairly, it is better to go back and try again rather than to take his chances, especially as there is no penalty against it. Now, suppose he has reached his front mark all right, and is going at the top of his speed toward the take-off. As he is reasonably sure of hitting the latter fairly, he can run ahead confidently, but he must not allow the length of his nine strides to the take-off to vary in the least; otherwise he will not strike it properly. It is not difficult to keep the strides even, as the athlete has only to run naturally, with the body bent well forward, the arms swinging regularly, and his sole thought that of jumping strongly on reaching the take-off. If he steps over the take-off even a few inches, his foot will sink into a hollow dug on the opposite side of the jumping-beam, and he will make what is called a foul, which counts as one of his trials. There is but little danger of spraining the ankle on a foul; that fear, therefore, should never be in mind, for it is liable to worry him out of his best performance. On the other hand, if the athlete fails to get up to the take-off, he must lose just as much of his jump. This is because his jump is not the actual distance he covers, but the distance from the opposite side of the take-off to the place where he first breaks ground in the jumping-box. Bearing these points in mind, he will see the necessity of compelling himself to keep cool, and will use his strength with greatest effect.

Now as to the act of jumping itself. Before the very last stride, and while running at the top of his speed, let the athlete gather himself together for the effort. He should bend his legs under him, get down as low as his high speed permits, fix his eye on some high distant object (to secure elevation), concentrate his strength in his back and hips, and then throw himself into the air. All these things are done in a flash, naturally, and not mechanically. It is necessary, however, to omit none of them if the athlete wishes really to out-do himself. Now, just as he hits the take-off, let him snap his right leg (if that is his jumping-leg) up as high as he can, and then push it down on the take-off with all his power, at the same time jerking both arms up quickly. The snap and push will lend the athlete additional power, and the jerk-up of the arms give elevation, an essential to a long jump. Just after leaving the take-off, let him curl the legs under his body, bend the head forward, and hold the arms rigidly at the side with every muscle in the body perfectly taut, so that his own weight will not bring him down immediately. Then, as he feels himself about to land, he should have sufficient presence of mind to kick his legs forward, bend the head still further over, and alight in that position. These latter movements will add a few inches to the jump, and that is what he needs. It will be seen that the jump is over in a few seconds, and the athlete may at first fail to act on all these suggestions. Repeated trials, however, will impress them upon him, and in a little time he will find himself observing them, almost without thinking.

It is well that the athlete should acquaint himself with the act of landing; that is, lighting in the jumping-box. The method I use is to land with my feet together; thereby obviating all danger of losing my balance, falling back, and spoiling my jump. The athlete should also steady himself for a moment after landing, and get out of the dirt feet first, breaking the layer of dirt no more than is absolutely necessary. A little care may mean several inches to the jump. Finally, it is also well for the athlete to see to it that the measurements are correct.

In conclusion, perhaps it is not out of place to make a few general remarks as to the broad jump. The athlete should remember never to jump without first limbering himself by a brisk dash, for he runs the liability of snapping a cord, and forever ruining himself for competition. He should not jump his best on the first trial unless he has been allowed several preliminary jumps. But on the second trial let him go in to win; and, if he gets a place in the finals, strive to improve on every effort. If possible, the athlete should keep his head, even under the most trying circumstances; because the moment he becomes rattled his skill departs, and actual strength counts for little. Half a dozen jumps twice a week should be sufficient to keep a man in form; and a complete rest of three or four days before a competition (provided the period of training has been rather long) is oftentimes the best thing that can be done. It is a good plan also for the athlete sometimes to do "staying-up" work, running, say, a brisk quarter of a mile once a week. On days when he is not jumping, the training need only consist in running short dashes in order to get up speed. As to diet, it need not be so heroic with the jumpers as with athletes whose work depends more on real power and less on nervous strength; if he keeps his stomach in good condition, and does not partake too freely of liquids, he should be able to jump without exhaustion and in good form.

Such is the method which I have followed, and such are the various observations that experience in competition for several years enables me to make. I can see no reason why others, with fairly strong natural ability and aptitude for jumping, should not be fully as successful as I have been, or perhaps beat the record that I have been able to make.

# SKATING.

### BY CHARLES R. TALBOT.

FOR your first lesson in skating, choose a piece of ice of moderate roughness. Take plenty of time to learn to stand well and safely on your skates, and to get confidence. Your danger as to falling is not, remember, of falling to one side, but backward or forward. Learn to stand up *straight*. There is nothing so awkward as a skater who leans forward. Avoid, too, swinging the arms about. They should be carried easily, much as in walking. Keep the feet close together, toes turned out, and the legs straight and firm.

Having come to feel somewhat at home upon your skates, and being able, perhaps, to move about a little, you may begin at once upon the Plain Forward Movement. With the left foot firmly planted, the inner edge of its skate bearing a little on the ice, boldly throw out the right foot until the outer edge of its skate touches the ice. At the same time throw the right shoulder steadily forward, and keep the body balanced upon the right leg as long as possible. Then throw out the left leg and shoulder in the same manner, and so continue. If you begin with these rules well in your head, it will save you much painful experimenting. Having learned to make progress in this manner with firmness and power, you will have learned to *skate*. Any other movement, simple or complex, belongs to " Fancy Skating." But, first of all, this plain stroke must be thoroughly learned.

The "rolls" forward and backward are the basis of all fancy skating. The forward outside-edge roll is made as follows: The impetus is obtained as in plain skating; but, as the stroke is made with the right foot, the left shoulder is brought forward, the right arm drawn back, and with the face looking to the right, the whole body is swung easily in the direction of the stroke; then the left foot is lifted from the ice, and, being brought forward, is set down a few inches in advance of the right. The same movement is then made to the left, the right skate having now its inner edge to the ice until ready to be lifted. The Dutch roll is performed in

*At Home on Skates.*

this same manner, save that, perhaps, the roll is not quite so broad, the movement being more nearly in a straight line. The marks left upon the ice are something as in the figure.

The outer-edge roll leads very easily to the cross roll, each foot when off the ice being swung, in the latter, *across* the one on the ice and starting in its stroke from the crossed position.

Having become proficient in the various rolls forward and backward, the skater is now prepared to

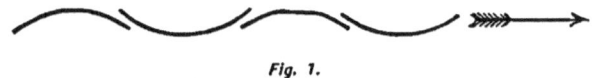

Fig. 1.

attempt for himself the almost infinite number of figures and movements that make up the rest of fancy skating. Most of these will require long practice. They are, too, for the most part, almost impossible to be described upon paper. You will have to pick them out for yourself, getting what helps you may from those about you who have already acquired them.

A favorite movement, and one easily mastered, is that which used to be familiarly known as "Cutting the Derby." It is now spoken of as the "Left-over-

Right," or the "Right-over-Left," and consists in skating in a circle by constantly putting the outside foot over forward and inside of its fellow. A few steps of this figure, thrown in now and then, first to one side and then to the other, makes a very graceful and easy variation of the plain forward roll.

Fig. 2.

"Cutting the Crab" is another simple figure. While going forward, one foot is suddenly thrown out, turned and drawn heel foremost directly after the other; and the greater part of a circle is then described, the two heels being brought close together and the toes turned straight outward. This is a neat way of coming to a stop if one has plenty of room.

The "Figure of Three" and the "Figure of Eight" have always been well known to skaters. The former begins at exactly the same point at which one would begin in writing the figure, and is performed on one foot, the

Fig. 3.

first part on the outside edge forward, and the second on the inside edge backward. The "Figure of Eight" is a combination of two circles. A very pretty "Rosette" is made by combining a number of "Figure of Eights," as seen in the figure. In this "Rosette," it will be observed, the first circle of the first "Eight" is gone over again and again, though the second one is constantly changed.

Then, there are all the other Arabic numerals to be made, and all the letters of the alphabet, if one

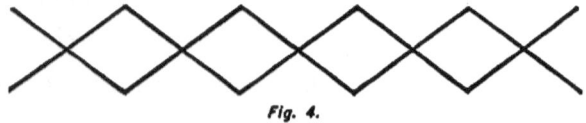

*Fig. 4.*

be patient and skilful enough. And there is the "Scissors," and the "Grapevine Twist," and the "Virginia Fence," which leaves a mark upon the ice that describes itself, and the "Locomotive," single and double, so called, doubtless, because the sound of its strokes somewhat resembles the puffings of an engine, and whose track is something as here seen; and there is the "On to Richmond" (cross one foot in front of the other, and with back stroke outside edge go backward or forward); and ever so many others.

You should see a programme for a skating contest as set forth by the American Skating Congress. I can assure you that the skaters who carry off the prizes from such contests must indeed be

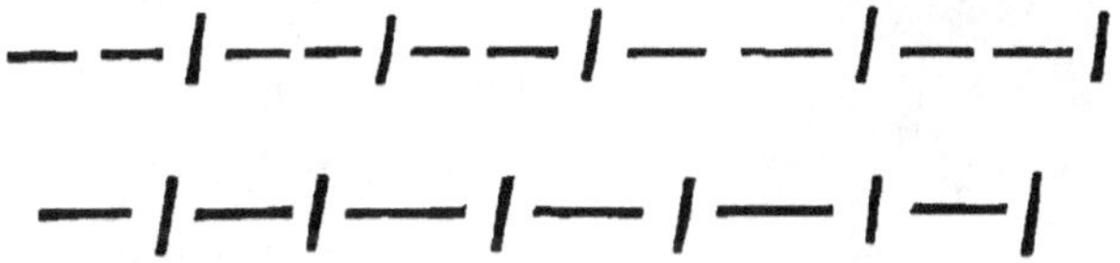

— —|— —|— —|— — —|— —|
— |— |— |— |— |— |

**Fig. 5.**

*artists*. And if you could only get hold of one of these Prize Skaters, and he would go to the pond with you, he could teach you more of Fancy Skating in half an hour upon the ice than I could do upon paper in half a year.

# HAND-IN-HAND SKATING.

### BY W. G. VAN T. SUTPHEN.
*From Harpers' Round Table.* Copyright, 1895, by Harper & Brothers.

THERE can be no lasting interest in any form of sport unless some definite end is kept in view, some problem finally worked out, some purpose accomplished. There is no amusement in shooting arrows aimlessly into the air, or in carelessly knocking tennis-balls over a net. The archer is intent on seeing how often he can hit the gold; the tennis-player tries to put that ball over in such a way that his opponent cannot return it. The score, the game — *something* is the object.

Now, skating is one of the oldest and most popular of winter amusements, and yet how many of the thousands of boys and girls who anxiously await the hoisting of the "red ball" know anything more than the merest beginnings of the art? The vast majority of skaters are perfectly satisfied with being able to progress in an aimless, desultory fashion up and down the ice, and keep out of the way of the hockey-players. And I may add that, good game though it is, hockey is not skating, in the real sense of the word; and it can never help you to anything better than the ability to keep your feet (and your temper) in a rough-and-tumble scrimmage after a little block of wood or a rubber "puck." And yet there is something better.

Aside from speed-skating, in which few can hope to excel, there is figure-skating, as it is popularly called. It is generally supposed to be very difficult, and in some respects it is so. To attempt it without the assistance of a teacher requires unlimited pluck and perseverance. There are a number of books on the subject, illustrated with elaborate diagrams, and everything made easy in theory. But the actual thing in practice—that is very different! It is like "French at Home, in Six Easy Lessons," or, "The Violin without a Master." The hard work does pay in the end, if persevered in; but the beginner generally gets disgusted after the first few failures, and goes back to tag and hockey. Perhaps that has been your experience — you have tried, and found it of no use; and yet you do envy the expert skater, who glides past you on the "back cross-roll" so easily and gracefully that you are certain that it must feel like flying. Well, that is exactly what it does feel like, and I am going to suggest a plan by which you may secure that delightful sensation for yourself at the expense of comparatively little time and trouble. After you have once known the fascination that there is in true figure-skating, you will probably feel encouraged to take up again the explanations and diagrams of the discarded text-books.

Hand-in-hand figures are among the prettiest things that can be done upon the ice from the spectators' point of view, and they are easiest for the performers. You have the assistance of your partner at every critical moment; and movements such as the forward-rocking turn, which require weeks of practice to do alone, can be executed hand in hand with comparative ease. In individual figure-skating you are obliged to advance very slowly in order to preserve correct form; in hand-in-hand skating the "form" is of less importance, or, rather, it seems to come of itself.

Let us take the "Mercury," or 3-scud as the English call it. If you will analyze the movements in the "Forward Mercury" (Fig. 3), you will see that there is first a glide on the left-foot outside edge backward (L.O.B.), then a glide forward on the right-foot outside edge (R.O.F.), and finally a cross-roll on the left-foot outside edge forward (L.O.F.), which finishes in a little backward turn on the same foot, leaving you in position to repeat the movement with the right foot on the outside edge backward (R.O.B.). Examining in like manner the detail of the "Backward Mercury" (Fig. 4), which is done by your partner at the same time that you are performing the "Forward," you will notice that it is exactly the same, except that there are *two* backward glides and *one* forward, while in the "Forward" there are *two* forward glides and *one* backward.

It is necessary, then, that both you and your partner should be able to skate the outside edge forward and back and make the little curl-like turn, and also that one of you should be reasonably proficient on the cross-roll backward. It sounds very difficult, but remember that I am not asking you to attempt all this alone: the secret lies in the fact that you will help each other.

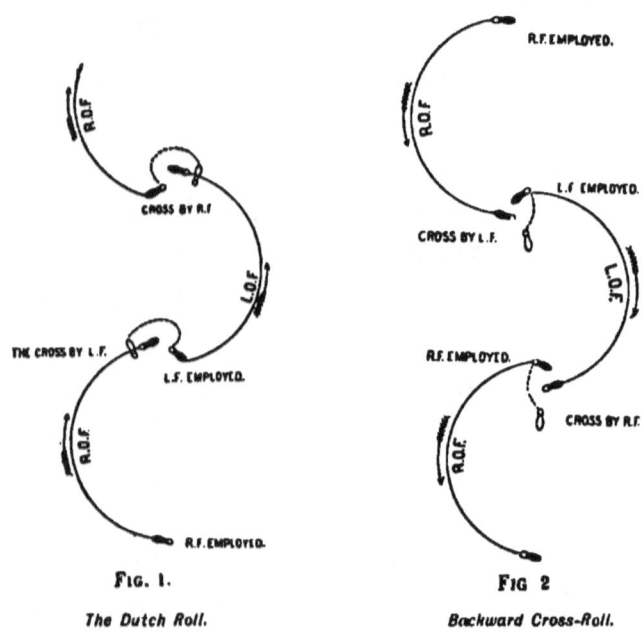

Fig. 1.  
The Dutch Roll.

Fig 2  
Backward Cross-Roll.

The outside edge forward is the first movement to be attempted. Try it with hands joined and crossed, and endeavor to make the stroke together — that is, in the same time. Lean boldly outward, and make the curve as long as possible. Try it again, but this time hand in hand, that is, with one hand free. It will be well to change sides occasionally.

Now for the same edge in a backward direction. To put the first question in the catechism to a very practical use, and to simplify the explanation, I will assume that you are M and that your partner is N. Join hands (not crossed), and let M try the outside backward on alternate feet, while N keeps both feet on the ice and simply squirms along in a serpentine line, and helps M to preserve his balance. M can then perform the same kindly office for N.

The only difference between the outside forward and the corresponding cross or Dutch roll (Fig. 1) is that the unemployed foot, instead of being put down alongside of the employed, is swung entirely over, and set down in front of the foot on which you have been gliding, and which is then immediately taken up. Join hands (not crossed), and let N skate backward, keeping both feet firmly on the ice. M will then follow on the outside forward, remembering to cross the unemployed foot just at the end of the glide. After the unemployed foot is swung over and put down, lift the other quickly

On the Ice.
(From the painting by J. S. Sargent.)

and let it swing gently out over the ice, and then bring it in ready for the next cross. You will soon find that you will not have to push off as you did on the ordinary outside edge; the swing of the unemployed leg is quite sufficient to bring you around.

Now for N's part, the backward cross-roll (Fig. 2), which is not quite so easy. As before, M will keep both feet on the ice, so as to give his partner a firm support. Join hands (not crossed), and let N take several backward steps as though he (or she) were walking, but crossing his feet alternately, the one behind the other, and turning the skate so that the outer edge is the one placed on the ice. After seven or eight steps, press the blade firmly into the ice as you set it down so that you can feel it "bite." Now give the unemployed leg a swing as you take it up; let it come all the way around, so that you can put it down (on the outside edge) well crossed behind the employed foot. Lean out as you do this, and let the skate that is on the ice move freely. Your partner can help you immensely if he will lift up on your hands, and at the same time gently force you over in the proper direction. It will seem impossible at first; but the knack will come all in a flash, and you will realize that it is the twist of your shoulders and the swing of the unemployed leg that is doing the work. It is very necessary to get these for-

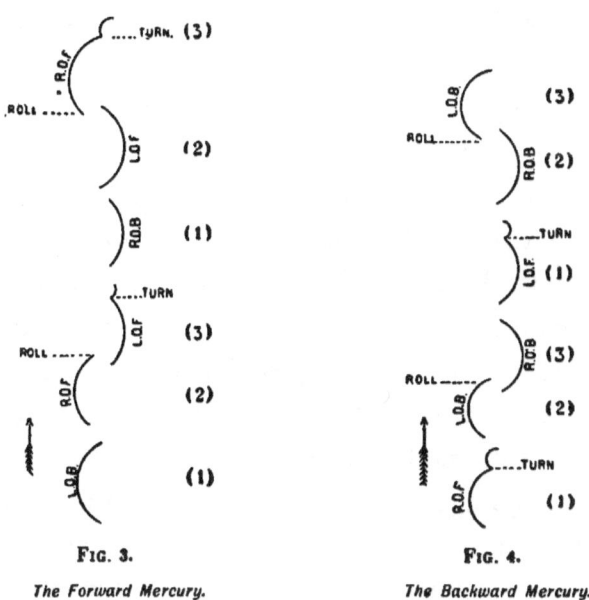

Fig. 3.
*The Forward Mercury.*

Fig. 4.
*The Backward Mercury.*

ward and back cross-rolls as perfect as possible before attempting the "Mercury" proper. Unless you can do them, the pace quickly gets too fast and dangerous, and the figure is spoiled.

There is only one thing more before we begin to put our material together, and that is the little turn on the same foot, which is technically called a "3." This particular turn is very easy, and is the natural one that everybody uses. Make the end or tail short, and practise on each foot forward and back.

As soon as M can be sure of his forward cross-roll, and N of the corresponding backward movement, we can try the whole figure. We will suppose that M has learned the "Forward," and N the "Backward." If anything, the "Backward" is the lady's step, as her partner should do the steering. Join hands (not crossed) and stand facing each other. Endeavor to take the strokes together in exactly the same time. You will find it of advantage to count one, two, three, as in learning the waltz. For instance, in the "Backward," begin on the right outside forward, and turn a "3" (count *one*), drop on the left outside back (*two*), cross the right foot behind, and continue on the right cross-roll backward (*three*). If, now, you are looking over your left shoulder, as you should on a right outside back, you will be ready for the left outside forward, ending with a "3" (*one*), the drop on to the right outside back (*two*), and the cross-roll backward on the left foot (*three*). The counting is the same for M, who does the " Forward ; " but he (or she) should be particular to see that his cross-roll forward (in which he makes the "3") is done in exactly the same time that N is doing the cross-roll back. The steering can be brought to as high a degree of perfection as in a ballroom. A variation of this figure, called the " Flying Mercury," is sometimes skated, the difference being that the skaters do not make the little turn or "3," but jump from one edge to another. It is very much more difficult, and should not be attempted without long practice on the regular figure. After you have become proficient in skating the " Mercury" with a partner, you can do the two movements by yourself. The " Forward" is particularly effective when done alone.

There are many other hand-in-hand figures, such as " Double Mohawks," " Q Scuds," and " Rocking Turns," which look well, done hand in hand. If you once learn the " Mercury," and get a little insight into the fascinating mystery of figure-skating, you will be anxious to look them up in the books, or seek the assistance of some friendly expert.

If you have a file or the bound volume of *Harper's Young People* for 1892, look up the article on figure-skating, under date of March 8. It contains some valuable hints on skate-fastenings and foot-gear. Above all, don't use straps, or you will never be able to skate with confidence and freedom. It is not strength, but suppleness of ankle, that is required; and any ankle that is strong enough to walk on without turning is strong enough to skate with. Straps cramp the muscles and stop the circulation. Use heel-plates and a key-fastening at the sole, unless you can set aside a pair of shoes for skating only; in this case the foot-stock should be permanently attached to the boot by ordinary screws.

# KNOTS, HITCHES, AND SPLICES.

### BY CHARLES R. TALBOT.

ON land or on water every boy should know how to knot a rope, splice two pieces of rope together, or make the sort of hitch which will best serve his purpose.

The first thing to be sure of is the right way to fasten together two pieces of string or rope. That is a thing that some of us have to do twenty times a day; and it is quite probable that twenty times a day we do it wrong. Suppose that you wish to lengthen your fish-line, or add another ball to a kite-string: how will you do it? Shall you lay the two ends side by side, and then twist them together into a knot, just as your sister would make one in the end of her thread?

If you do, you may fairly expect that your fish will get away with the main part of your line, or that presently your kite will go skurrying off far out of your sight. Such a knot is at least as likely to slip as to hold, and, if tied in a rope, is liable sooner or later to cut the rope, because the strain is at right angles. What is really wanted is a Square-knot (Fig. 3, *a*).

Take the two ends, and tie them together exactly as you would tie a "hard-knot" in your shoe-string.

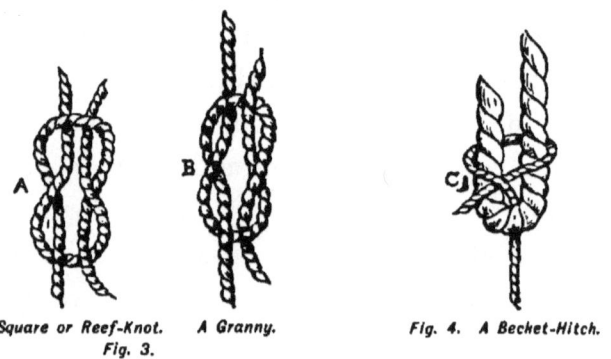

A Square or Reef-Knot.    A Granny.        Fig. 4. A Becket-Hitch.
Fig. 3.

Only you must be careful and not tie a Granny (Fig. 3, *b*). One *may* slip; the other won't.

Fig. 4 is a Becket-hitch, the proper knot for joining a large and a smaller rope. It will be useful, for example, when the keleg-line of your boat is too short, and the only line at hand to bend on to it is a stout piece of hemp twine.

A loop at the end of a rope — that is, a loop that will not draw up — is another knot that has frequently to be made. And yet few people know how to make it. What is wanted in such a case is a Bowline.

Make a bight near the end of your rope, as in the first cut of Fig. 5. Seize this with the left hand at *a*, and then with the right hand pass the end *b* up through the bight, around behind the main part of the rope at *c*, and down in front of

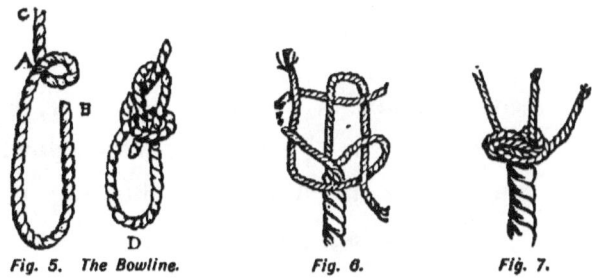

Fig. 5. The Bowline.   Fig. 6.   Fig. 7.

it through the bight again as in *d*. Draw this tight and you have the much-talked-of Bowline. It is a very simple matter, as you see.

While speaking still of the ends of ropes, let us stop and learn to "fasten them off" properly to prevent their untwisting or fraying out. The painter or main-sheet of your boat may need such treatment. The simplest method is to "serve" or wind the end with small twine. A Single-wall (Fig. 6), or a Double-wall (Fig. 7), is better. But better still is the Boatswain's-whipping, formed by making an inverted single-wall and then splicing the ends back over the rope itself (Fig. 8 and Fig. 9).

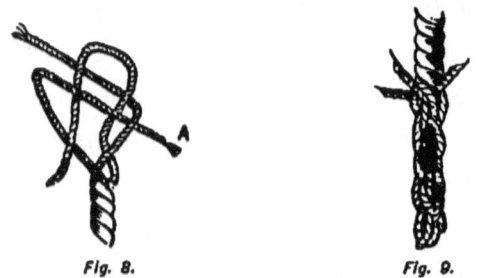

Fig. 8.    Fig. 9.

The most elegant of all such, however, is the Stopper-knot, seen in the four figures below.

Place the end *a* as in Fig. 10, holding it with

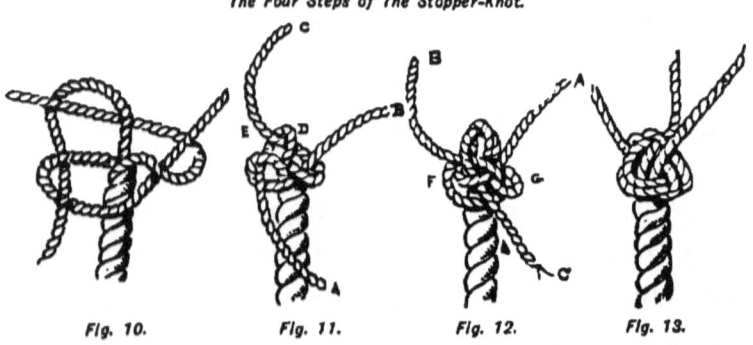

The Four Steps of The Stopper-Knot.

Fig. 10.    Fig. 11.    Fig. 12.    Fig. 13.

the thumb at *d*; pass *b* around under it, *c* around under *b* and through the bight of *a*, and pull tight; this forms a Single-wall (Fig. 11). Now lay *a* over *d*, *b* over *e*, *c* over *b* and through the bight of *a*, and draw tight (Fig. 12).

Next pass *b* down around *f* and up through the bight *g*, and do the same with *a* and *c*, forming Fig. 13.

Finally pass each strand by the side of the strands in the crown down through the walling to form the "double-crown," and cut close the ends *a*, *b* (and *c*), and you have produced the Stopper-knot.

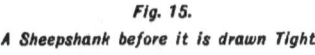

Fig. 15.
A Sheepshank before it is drawn Tight.   Fig. 16.   The True-Lover's Knot.

A Sheepshank (Fig. 15) is a knot by which a rope may be made shorter, or (as a young yachtwoman of my acquaintance recently expressed it) "a tuck taken in it." If the tide has come in and you wish to shorten the mooring-line of your boat, the Sheepshank will gather up the slack for you and hold it firmly.

When one wants to make an artificial handle for

an old jug or some other vessel, the True-Lover's knot is used, as seen in Fig. 16.

Tie two loose knots, *a*, *b*, as in the first cut of

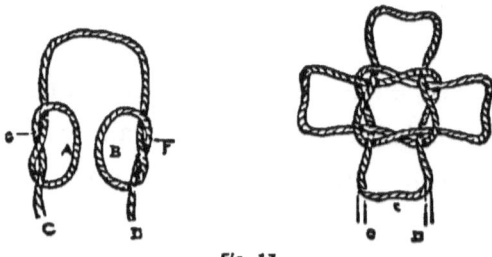

Fig. 17.

Fig. 17; pass the bight *a* through the opening *f*, the bight *b* through *g*, pull the loops equal, and, to complete the knot as in second cut of Fig. 17, join the ends *c*, *d*, by a long splice at *e*.

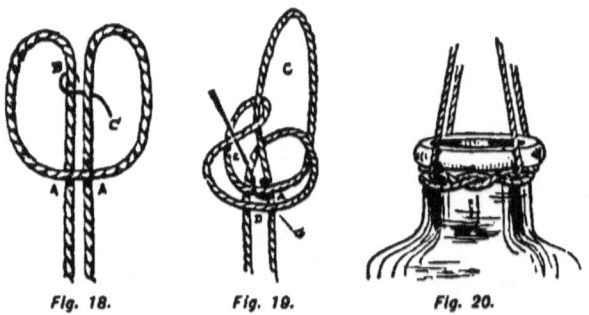

Fig. 18. Fig. 19. Fig. 20.

The Jar-sling, seen in Fig. 20, serves a similar purpose. In a long piece of cord, make a large loop as in Fig. 18, and hold the bight against the standing parts, *a*, *a*; pass the thumb and forefinger of the other hand down through *c*, lay hold of *b* where the crook of the imaginary wire is seen, and draw it through *c* down a little below *a*, *a*, as in Fig. 19, *d*, and hold it there. Now pass the thumb and forefinger down through the opening *e* (in the way the wire goes), lay hold of *g*, and draw it up through *e*, forming the complete knot as in Fig. 20.

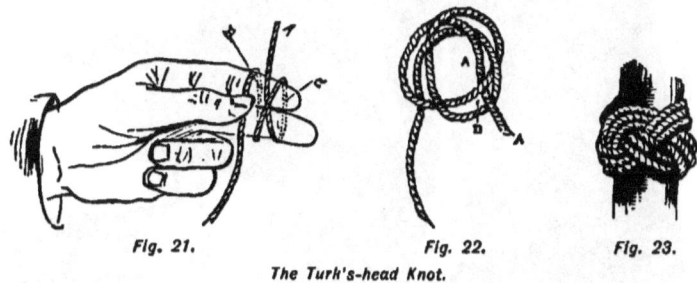

Fig. 21.       Fig. 22.       Fig. 23.
The Turk's-head Knot.

One more knot, the Turk's-head (Fig. 23), remains to be described before we pass to the briefer subject of hitches. Take a long piece of fishing-cord, place the end *a* against the forefinger, wind the cord around the two fingers and hold it with the thumb, as in Fig. 21.

Now with the other hand lay the part *b over* the part *c*, and while in that position pass the end *a* down between them, over the first crossing, under

Where a Hitch Comes Handy.

left strand, up between, over second crossing, under right strand, up between; take the hitch off your fingers, and it will be as in Fig. 22.

Next pass the loose end through the opening *d*, laying it against the cord *a*; then, with it, follow that strand (*a*) over and under, over and under, until you have a complete plait of three cords. Pass the knot over a stick to make it taut, and cut the ends close.

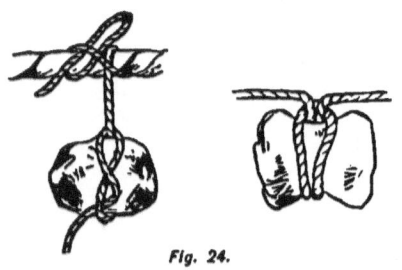

Fig. 24.
Two Ways of Fastening a Weight to a Line.

Fig. 25.
To Tie a Short Line, to which a Hook is Attached, to a Longer or Ground Line.

The Turk's-head knot, like the two preceding it, will tax your precision, deftness, and patience, and is an ornamental rather than a useful knot.

The knots in Figs. 24, 25, and 26 explain themselves; they are often useful to picknickers and campers-out.

*Hitches* are no less *knots* than any of the foregoing; but they are knots used to fasten the end of a rope to any object in such manner as to be easily cast off when no longer needed. They are few in number, and all very simple and easily described.

A Blackwall hitch is merely a loop thrown about a hook, as in Fig. 27, in such a way that the main part of the rope, *c*, being pulled downward, the part *a* jams the part *b* against the hook so firmly that while the strain is kept up the knot cannot possibly

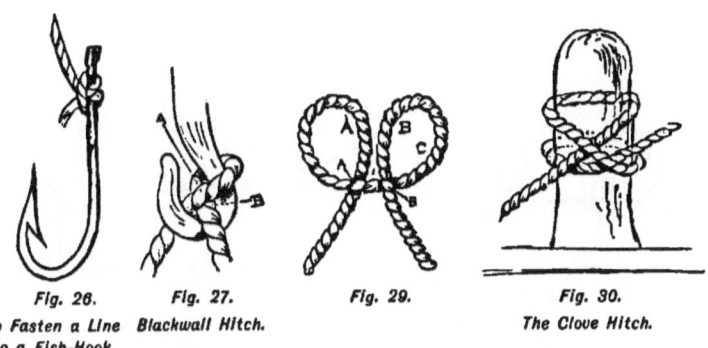

Fig. 26.    Fig. 27.      Fig. 29.      Fig. 30.
To Fasten a Line   Blackwall Hitch.           The Clove Hitch.
to a Fish-Hook.

slip. Sailors use this hitch very frequently; but it can be used on land as well as at sea.

Of all hitches, however, the one which any man or boy can least afford not to know is the Clove hitch. Make two bights or loops, as in Fig. 29; hold them between the thumbs and forefingers at *a*, *b*; slide the left loop over the right loop; then slip the double loop thus formed over the table-leg, or anything that will represent a post, and draw tight by the end (Fig. 30). Practise this until your fingers can do it swiftly and of themselves, just as your tongue can say the alphabet; for a Clove hitch, when it is used, needs to be made quickly and handsomely. I once saw a young cadet from Annapolis, who had been out on a sailing-party with some ladies, and had jumped ashore with a rope, hesitate

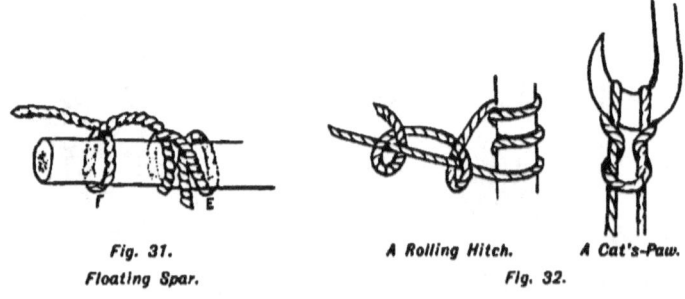

Fig. 31.
Floating Spar.

A Rolling Hitch.
Fig. 32.

A Cat's-Paw.

at least half a minute before he could think how to make the proper knot, while a number of old sea-captains sitting by were watching him and laughing among themselves. A Clove hitch may be used, too, when, while out fishing, you extemporize an anchor by tying a rope to a stone. And in Fig. 31 you see again how this knot, $e$ (with a half-hitch, $f$, in front of it), is used to tow a floating spar, or drag a piece of timber across the field.

Two other hitches, a Rolling hitch and a Cat's-paw, are shown in Fig. 32.

Splicing is a process by which ropes are joined together so as to leave no knot. I appreciated its importance one morning when I saw an intelligent man of fifty work for an hour to splice a hammock rope. Where it is not specially important that the joining be a very nice and smooth one, the "short" splice is used. It is made by passing the strands of one piece in and out between those of the other. The short splice always leaves the spliced part thicker and clumsier than the rest of the rope. If it is desirable that the joining be a very neat one, so as to admit of the rope's running readily through the sheave-hole of a block, the "long" splice is necessary. This is made by unwinding each end about two inches, placing the strands as in the short splice, then unwinding one strand farther back, and winding the corresponding strand of the other piece in its place; proceeding in the same way with the other strands, and then fastening the ends in such a way that it is almost impossible to detect the splice. We have not space to describe here the exact mode of procedure; but there is scarcely a town or village anywhere but has its "old sailor," and there is no old sailor anywhere but will be glad to come and give you a lesson in splicing.

A splice that you can very easily learn for yourselves, however, is the Eye-splice. First make yourself a marling-spike, — if you have not the genuine article, — by whittling down to a point a piece

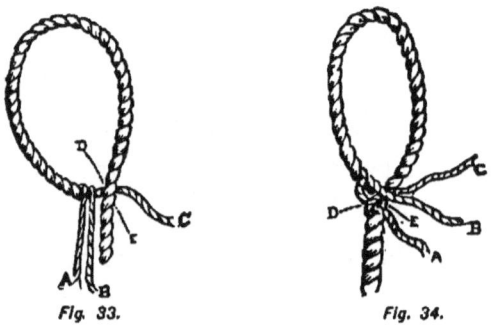

Fig. 33.  Fig. 34.

of hard wood. I have found that the half of a clothes-pin, so treated, answered the purpose exceedingly well. Then take a piece of good three-strand rope, unwind the strands, and place them as you see, *a, b, c,* in Fig. 33. Open the strand *d,* and pass *a* through it, as in Fig. 34; then open *e,* and pass *b over d* and *under e,* as in Fig. 35. Turn the eye over, Fig. 36, open *f* and pass *c* through it, as in Fig. 37, and pull the strands tight. Now pass *a over* the strand next it, *under* the next one, and so on with the others. Proceed in the same way until the splice is about an inch long. Then stretch the eye (holding by the rope), to tighten everything, and cut the ends close. If you will make a neat

Fig. 35.   Fig. 36.   Fig. 37.

Eye-splice all by yourself, and take it to the old sailor aforementioned, he will be sure to think it worth while to teach you all he knows; and he will be likely to tell you many things about knots, hitches, and splices which are of necessity omitted here.

## SUMMER SPORTS.

#### BY THE EDITOR.

SUMMER at last. Bright summer, glad summer, delightful summer, jolly summer, as different poets have called it. The sun lies warm on the open uplands, the breeze blows soft across the grassy valleys, the shady spots upon the edges of the rustling wood look cool and inviting; and so, out of the sun and into the shadow let us pass, accepting the invitation of still another famous poet —

> "Under the greenwood tree,
> Who loves to lie with me
> And tune his merry note
> Unto the sweet bird's throat,
> Come hither, come hither, come" —

But what! cry all our would-be athletes in chorus; loll under the trees like cows and other cattle for sheer laziness and cud-chewing? No, sir, not we. Summer means fun, and not loafing. It means the open air and the blue sky; it means the freedom of street and park and meadow and seashore, and all the big playground that Mrs. Nature has laid out for the young people who seek her. So, sir, under no trees and into no shadows do we go while there are enough of us stirring to get up some jolly, good game, or take sides in some particularly favorite fun.

I suppose there never was a nation, race, or people since first the earth was made, that did not have girls and boys who not only loved play, but did play, and with a will. The Eskimos of the frozen North, the Tupinambras of the Brazilian pampas, the *gamins* of the Paris streets, the boys and girls of London and Boston and New York, have in their nature one kindred tie,—the love of sport.

But if there is any boy or girl who thinks that he or she has ever conceived, planned, or played a new game, let such consider well before claiming the right of invention.

There is nothing new under the sun, said the wise man; and especially is there nothing new in young folks' games. Archæologists find well-beloved dolls in Egyptian pyramids and on pre-

*A Challenge.*

historic tombs; the name of a popular ball-club was found scrawled upon the outer walls of Pompeiian houses; and one of the most exciting base-ball matches on record was the one, stubbornly fought, between the rival nines of Montezuma, King of Mexico, and Nezahualpilli, 'tzin of Tezcuco. The boys of ancient Greece and Rome played at whip-top and quoits, and base-ball and pitch-penny, and blind-man's-buff and hide-and-seek, and jack-stones and follow my leader, just as do the boys of to-day; the girls were experts at see-saw, and swinging and dancing, and grace-hoops and dice-throwing and ball-play, and, in Sparta, even at running, wrestling, and leaping. Tobogganing is as old as ice and snow; and when you play at cherry-pits you are only doing what Nero and Commodus and young Themistocles did ages ago in Rome and Athens.

So, whatever the age or clime, the boys and girls of the world have always lived more for play than anything else; and however harsh or hard their surroundings, however stern or strict their fathers and mothers, they always found and made the most of the time for play, and, more than any other season, the time for summer sports.

These sports to-day are fast reducing themselves into as many sciences, over-weighted with rules and restrictions, that often take the real play element from them, and make them as unyielding and sedate as a problem in algebra.

Now, while rules and restrictions are undoubtedly necessary, there is such a thing as going too far; and I am inclined to believe that the boys and girls prefer to follow the cast-iron rules only to the verge of "cast-ironness," and make their sport, if less absolute, at least more jolly. There is no fun in making our sport a matter of life and death.

I know grown people who, in these days of prize-giving in all manner of games, centre their whole desires, not on the fun of the game, but on the prizes offered. They really seem as disappointed if they do not carry off a trophy as if they had met with some serious loss. Let us take our fun with jollity or not at all. Interest is one thing, and irritability is quite another.

So, whatever the game you are playing, remember that the best of all rules is: Keep your temper. Life has plenty of shifting clouds without the necessity of quarrels over games; disputes and bickerings have far too often broken up a

*"Tobogganing is as Old as Ice and Snow."*

merry company, and spoiled the beauty of a summer play-day.

Now, while I fully realize that no new games are likely to supplant foot-ball, base-ball, or tennis in the favor of Young America, I do feel sure that there is left plenty of room for some such games as may be played by any number of young people, — boys or girls, — and without the necessity of having carefully prepared grounds. Croquet formerly filled this want; and golf, called by one enthusiast "a sort of glorified croquet," is at present attracting a good deal of attention. But croquet has fallen more or less into disfavor, and golf can be played only in the open country. For this reason I am going to say just a word about one or two games which may be played almost anywhere by any number of people.

And in the first of these — the good old English game of bowls — the croquet balls which have been unused for several years may be made to do service.

The "bowls" used in the scientific game are peculiarly constructed, but for unprofessional sport the croquet balls will serve the purpose. The rules here given are for this unprofessional game, and are those pronounced by a very recent au-

The Old-fashioned Game of Bowls.

thority on this attractive sport. Retain the sides chosen for your last game of croquet, and let the captains choose for "first." The ground is marked off by a line at one end, and a small quoit is placed in the centre of a ring at the other. The game is commenced by the first player of the side winning the toss; he endeavors to roll his ball as near as possible to the quoit, or tee as it is called. The first player on the other side then strives to roll his ball either closer to the tee than is that of his adversary, or, if that is not possible, to drive his opponent's ball away. If he fails to do either, then the second player of the leading side rolls his ball so as to guard the first player's ball from attack; and so the game proceeds until all the balls have been rolled to the tee, when the side whose ball or balls are nearest to the tee scores an ace for each ball counting. Only the side to whom belongs the ball nearest the tee can count; so, if the second nearest ball is an opponent's, the winning side can only count one. The winner of the game is the side which first scores twenty-one. Should a ball settle in the centre of the tee quoit, then the count is four, unless the ball be knocked off the quoit, either by an opponent's ball, or by a ball of the side which rolled it on the tee. These are the rules for a bowling court or field with one end. If two ends are laid out, two tees or quoits are set one at either end, and the contestants roll from each end alternately.

One of the most fascinating in the whole list of summer sports is canoeing. There is, indeed, no reason why a boy who can swim should not paddle his own canoe without assistance or watching. Mr. John Habberton tells a story of offering a watch and chain to one of his boys if he could prove himself able to upset a canoe while sitting in the bottom. Mr. Habberton declares that he saved both the watch and the boy; for the canoe could not be tipped over.

Canoe-racing has perhaps injured quite as much as it has benefited the sport of canoe-cruising. The racers have devised improvements in model and in rig, of which the canoeists who do not race have taken advantage; but they have contrived by their recklessness in carrying too much sail, and by the upsets which naturally follow, to foster a public impression that the canoe is a cranky craft. This, as may be learned from Mr. Habberton's experience, is not the case.

The regulation canoe is decked over, except where the small well-hole appears in the centre. Waves of ordinary size, therefore, cannot break over the coverings.

The limited crew of a canoe should always sit

*The Canoeist's Landing.*

upon the bottom of the craft. The canoe, if thus handled, will be found remarkably free from rolling, and, being furnished with air-tight compartments, nearly as safe as an ordinary row-boat.

It is difficult to fill or swamp a well-built and properly managed canoe, and it is impossible to sink her when full. She will outride any form of row-boat, and will live through a storm in which a small steam-launch will go down.

The cost of a canoeist's outfit varies all the way from ten to four hundred dollars; but just as much fun and exercise can be had with a home-made affair or a cheap canoe as with the most elegant boat in the market, rich in polished mahogany and Spanish cedar, and glittering with silver-plating.

Girls, as well as boys, make expert canoeists; and the sport is healthful, safe, and altogether delightful.

As a capital game of strength and skill, played at many a jolly picnic and on many a shady stretch of lawn or level ground, the game of Quoits has for generations proved a source of interest, enjoyment, and friendly rivalry.

Quoits is but a modern adaptation of the old Grecian game of Throwing the Discus.

There is, however, this difference: the *discus* was a much heavier ring than is the modern quoit; and the object of the old Greek game was to determine which *discobolus* had the stronger arm, and could throw his *discus* farthest. In Quoits the object is to place the quoit nearest a certain fixed point.

The iron rings are thrown at the pin, or "hob," placed from forty to sixty feet away. The object is

*The Quoit Thrower.*
*(Copy of the Marble of the Discobolus of the Vatican.)*

to ring the hob, — a task rarely accomplished, — or to get as near to the hob as possible.

Players may throw alternately, or sides may be chosen. Each player throws all his quoits; and when all have been cast an investigation is made. If A (supposing him to have thrown three quoits) has placed his three nearer the hob than has B, he counts three toward the total score. If one of his is nearest the hob, and B owns the next nearest, then A can count but one, no matter how closely to the hob his other quoits may lie. The same rule holds good in playing sides.

When the count has been determined, the players stand at the hob first played at, and throw their quoits at a hob driven in at the starting-point. This alternate playing is continued until the full score has been made by one side or player. The total score is twenty-one. If a quoit rings the hob, — that is, completely encircles it, — the successful pitcher counts ten.

The "science" in Quoits consists in careful throwing. Hold the flat side of the quoit downward, with the forefinger resting in the notch and the thumb on the upper side. Give the quoit a spinning motion with the forefinger, so that it will fall with its edge downward, cutting its way into the ground, with its flat side toward the thrower. The quoit may be best aimed by sighting the hob through the hole in the centre. Don't throw the quoit so that it will "wobble," and not stick in the ground, or so that its flat side is up. This last is sometimes counted as a dead quoit, and has no claim in the score.

The throwers may grow tired before the game is over; but it is a "healthy tired" if the distances are not too great, and the sport is one fitted to strengthen the muscles and train the eyes of strong-limbed boys and girls.

An exciting, though sometimes a rather rough game for the boys to play is "Ball in the Hole," or "Nine Holes" as it is sometimes called. The simple description taken from the "American Boys' Book of Sports" fully describes a game that is as popular among the street-boys of New York as among the boys who have plenty of space and elbow-room in the open and breezy country.

"Dig near a wall," says the "Boys' Book," "nine holes of about six inches in diameter and three deep. Let each player have one of these, according to his number, which must be determined by lot. At about six yards from the holes draw a line; and from this, as a fielding-place, one player pitches the ball into one of the holes.

"The boy to whom this hole is assigned immediately runs to it, while all the players run off in different directions.

"The player snatches the ball from the hole, and throws it at one of the runners. If he hits him, the boy thus struck becomes the pitcher, and the one that struck him counts one. Should he not hit him, the player who throws the ball loses a point, and bowls.

"The player who misses his aim at throwing the ball at his partners a second time, becomes a 'tenner.' If he loses the third hit, he is a 'fifteener;' if the fourth, he stands out and can play no more."

When all the players are thus out, the last player remaining in wins the game; and he can compel each of the losers to stand against the wall and be "peppered" by the successful player with the ball used in the game. This "peppering" should, however, be done mildly, if at all; for a victor should always remember to be moderate in his hour of victory.

Moderation is good in all things — in summer sports as well as in winter work. But competition is also healthy; and if there be thus a genuine, whole-souled attempt, on the part of all the boys who admire physical strength and prowess, to allow only the good and ennobling influences in their play to work upon their characters, then I am sure that they will be "backed up" and encouraged by their elders in all the enthusiasm they show in that direction.

Athletics, in one form or another, are nearly as old as history itself; and the present attempt, under the encouragement of several college professors, to revive the Olympic games in Greece, indicates that students of history realize there is something more to be gained by such a gathering than the mere settling of a disputed championship. It rests, however, with the youth who engage actively in the contests to show what they are capable of doing in the strengthening of both body and character.

# INDEX.

"Athlete," the word, 11.
Athletics, the lessons of, 13; physical benefits of, 14; evils of, 16.

Ball in the Hole, 312.
Base-Ball: too professional, 33; planning for season's work, 34; training-time, 34; muscle developing, 34; practice work, 35; base sliding, 36; coaching, 37; selecting the pitchers, 37; the cage, 37; batting, 37; Easter trip, 38; table diet, 39; base running, 40; batters' running, 40; fearlessness, 40; infielders, 41; playing ahead, 41; coaching, 41.
Bicycles: need of good roads, 96; sidewalk riding, 97; politeness pays, 98; "scorching," 99; costumes for girls, 100; clothing, 108; the machine, 104; the cheapest of luxuries, 105.
Boating (see *Crew Training*).
Bowls, 303.
Boynton, Captain, 224.
Bliss of Yale (foot-ball), 25.

Butler, Dennis F. (swimmer), 194.

Cane Rush: not brutal, 226; the ground, 228; the cane, 228; a hand, 228; signals, 228; the Gladiatoræ, 228; the Robustæ, 228; the Avelli, 228; the Salturæ, 229; the Palæstræ, 229; costume, 230; the rush, 231; the scrimmage, 232; the decision, 235; the prize, 236.
Canoeing, 306.
Copeland, A. F., hurdler, 243, 248.
Crew Training: selection of men, 56; age of men, 57; training, 57; exercise, 58; gymnasium work, 59; avoid overdoing, 60; food while training, 60; sleep, 63; regularity, 64; time of preparation, 65; the stroke, 66, 68; shell-rowing, 66; the full reach, 67, 69; the catch, 70; the shoot, 70; rowing, 71; the rowing machine, 72; lifting, holding, and backing, 73; the stroke oarsmen, 73; weight of crew, 73; trimming, 73; objects of training, 73.

Cricket: first game of, in America, 76; the field, 76; the pitch, 76; stumps, 77; bails, 78; bowler's crease, 78; the bat, 78; arrangement of game, 79; the bowler, 79; the batsman, 80; placing the field, 81; bowling and pitching, 81.
Croquet, 303.
Crosby of Harvard (foot-ball), 25.

Dana, R. H., 186.
*Discus*, the, 308.

England and Australia Cricket Match, 82.

Foot-ball: how to develop a team, 21; blocking and kicking, 22; team play, 23; blocking and getting through, 24; tackling, 25; the tackle bag, 26; passing, 26; a back's duties, 26; warding off, 29; self coaching, 29; practice games, 30; team spirit, 30; "stars" no good, 30; responsibility of each man, 31; detail work, 31; signalling, 32; a champion eleven, 32.

Germantown Cricket Club, 82.
Golf: popularity of, 88; exercise in, 89; an all-the-year game, 89; space a requisite, 90; a full course, 90; the putting green, 90; the teeing ground, 91; the ball, 91; the game, 91; "honor," 92; a round, 92; singles, 92; a foursome, 93; a moderate golf equipment, 93.

Gymnastics: benefits of, 146; fresh air the chief tonic, 146; an out-of-door "gym," 147; the Charlesbank, 147; class drill, 148; the giant stride, 150; the neck developer, 151; the medicine ball, 151; the spring board, 152; the buck, 152; the tilting ladder, 152; the Jacob's ladder, 154; the "razzle dazzle," 154; a home gymnasium, 156; trapeze bar, 157; rings, 158; horizontal bar, 158; jumping standards, 162; vaulting-horse, 162.

Habberton, John, on canoeing, 306.
Hare and Hounds: the hares, 122; the hounds, 122; the master, 122; the scent, 122; the route, 122; prizes, 123; an ideal course, 123; the break; 125; endurance, 127.
Harvard Batting Team of '91, 37.
Haverford College, cricket at, 87.
Hand-in-Hand Skating (see *Skating*).
Hawks, Lord (cricket), 82.
Hitches (see *Knots, Hitches, and Splices*).
Hurdling: requirements for, 116; the spring, 117; distances, 117; the hurdles, 118; strides, 118; description of, 238; elements of a good hurdler, 241; striking the hurdles, 244; handicap races, 246, 249; "mug-hunters," 247; the "scratch" man, 248, 250; the "scratch" races, 250; the intercollegiate contests, 250.

INDEX.  317

Interscholastic tournaments, value of, 48.

Jordan, A. A., the hurdler, 244.
Jump, the Running Broad: the jumping path, 252; the jumping foot, 252; number of strides, 253; the marks, 253; the take-off, 254; a foul, 254; the jump, 255; landing, 256; caution and advice to jumpers, 257; training, 258.

Knots, Hitches, and Splices, 280; a square knot, 281; becket knot, 281; bowline, 252; single wall and double wall, 282; boatswain's whipping, 283; stopper knot, 283; sheepshank, 284; true-lover's knot, 285; jar sling, 285; Turk's head, 286; hitches, 289; Blackwall hitch, 290; clove hitch, 290; rolling hitch and cat's paw, 292; splicing, 292; the eye splice, 293.

Lake of Harvard (foot-ball), 29.
Lawn Tennis: not so easy as it looks, 43; value of tournaments, 48; choice of rackets, 50; balls, 51; a good stroke, 51; length of court, 52; fast service, 52; the volley, 52; hitting and "smashing," 55; odds, 55.
Longwood Cricket Club, 87.

Manheim Cricket Grounds, 85.
Mapes, of Columbia (hurdling), 238.
Moderation in sport, 314.
"Mug-hunters" (see *Hurdling*).

Newell of Harvard (foot-ball), 24.
Nine Holes (see *Ball in the Hole*).

Olympic Games, revival of, 314.
Over-training, 17.

*Pancratium* (see *Cane Rush*).
Paper Chase (see *Hare and Hounds*).
Pedestrian Exercise (see *Walking*).
Philadelphia, the home of American Cricket, 81.
Prize-giving in "sports," 300.

Quoits: the pin, 308; the hob, 308; science in, 311.

Roberts, Mr., Y. M. C. A. Gymnasium (Boston), 151.
Running: long legs not needed, 107; heart must be strong, 108; dashes, 109; training, 109; sprinting, 111; positions, 111; styles of starting, 112; the scratch, 112; style of running, 116. (See *Jump* and *Hurdling*.)
Running Broad Jump, The (see *Jump*).

St. Paul's School, cricket at, 87.
Sears, F. R. (tennis), 45.
Skating: first lessons in, 259; plain forward movement, 259; the rolls, 260; cutting the Derby (or left over right), 263; cutting the crab, 264; figure of three and of eight, 264; the rosette, 265; scissors, 265; grapevine twist, 265; Virginia fence, 265; on to Richmond, 265; hand-in-hand skating, 267; hockey

Skating, *continued*.
skating, 268; speed skating, 268; figure skating, 268; hand-in-hand figures, 269; the Mercury (forward and backward), 270, 277; backward cross-roll, 270, 275; the Dutch roll, 272; the flying Mercury, 278; double Mohawks, Q scuds, and rocking turns, 278; skate-fastenings and foot-gear, 279.

Sliding machine for base-ball, 36.

Splices (see *Knots, Hitches, and Splices*).

Stagg of Yale (base-ball), 36.

Summer Sports, 295; antiquity of, 296; rules and restrictions in, 300.

Surrey and Nottinghamshire Cricket Match, 82.

Swimming: confidence essential, 190; secret of a good stroke, 191; dog-fashion, 192; the breast stroke, 192; side stroke, 193; right-hand, left-hand, and overhand stroke, 193; back performances, 194; diving, 195; under-water swimming, 196; treading water, 199; other feats, 200; precautions, 201; a tub race, 203; a water circus, 206; water polo, 213; water shoes, 223.

Tennis (see *Lawn Tennis*).

Trafford of Harvard (foot-ball), 29.

Tub Race, A (see *Swimming*).

University of Pennsylvania, cricket at, 87.

Walking: value of, 128; time of a walking trip, 129; arranging route, 130; outfit, 131; clothing, 133; size of party, 137; eating, 138; out-of-door sleeping, 140; routes suggested, 143; have an object, 145.

Water Circus, A (see *Swimming*).

Water Polo (see *Swimming*).

Water Shoes (see *Swimming*).

Winter of Yale (foot-ball), 25.

Yachting: the compass, 166; taking a bearing, 173; keeping the course, 174; management, 175; fair-weather sailing, 176; in an emergency, 176; sea-terms, 179–186; starboard and port, 187–189.

www.ingramcontent.com/pod-product-compliance
Lightning Source LLC
Chambersburg PA
CBHW022023240426
43667CB00042B/1071